FLEMISH ILLUMINATED MANUSCRIPTS

1400–1550

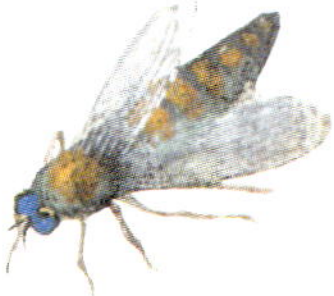

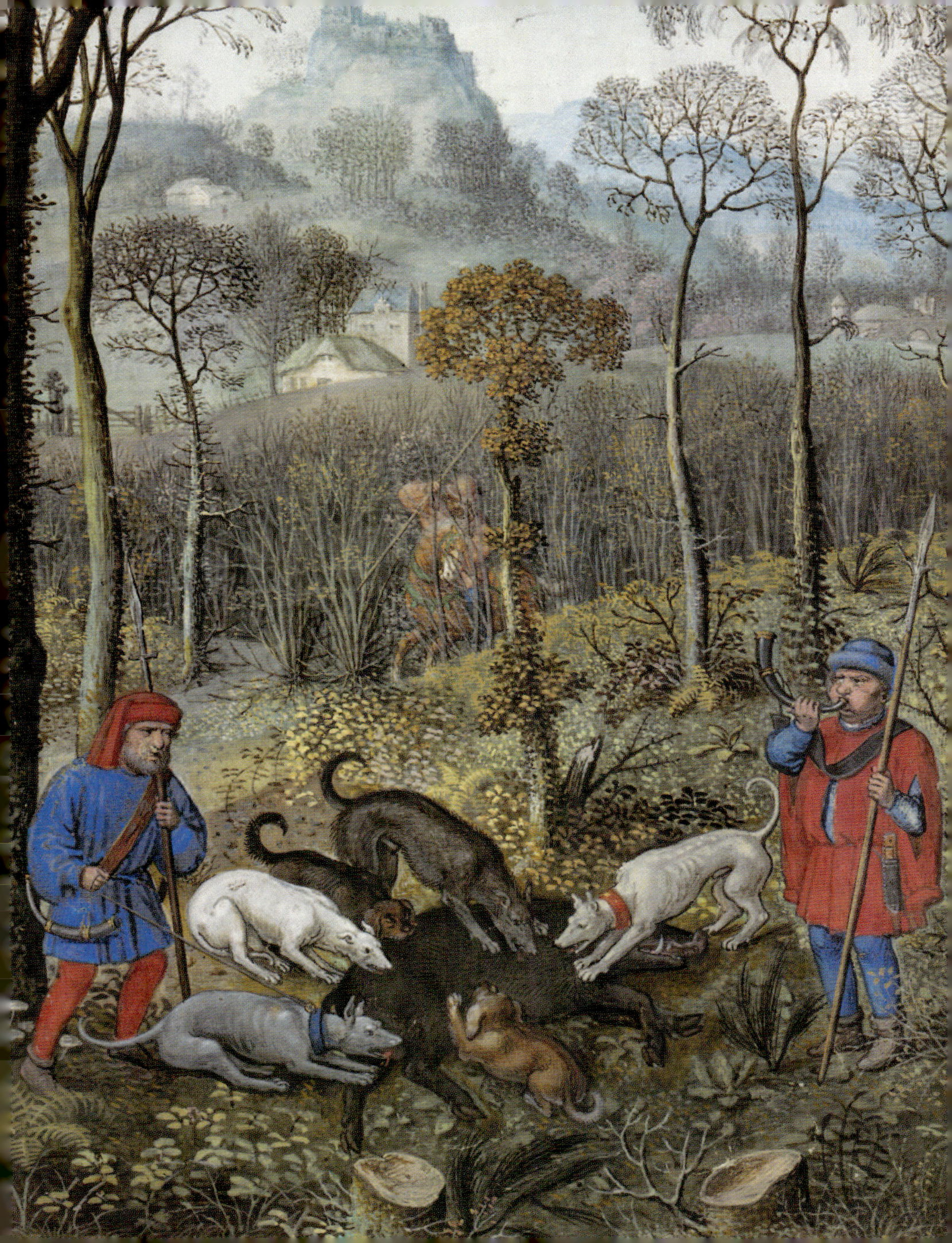

FLEMISH ILLUMINATED MANUSCRIPTS

1400–1550

Scot McKendrick

THE BRITISH LIBRARY

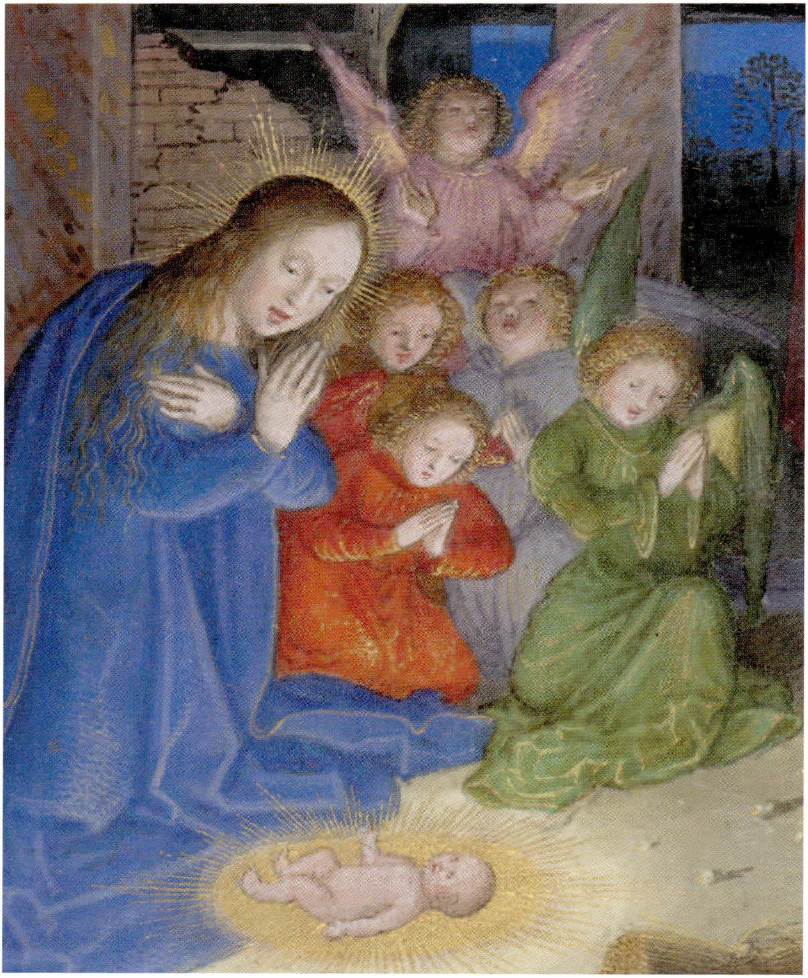

FRONTISPIECE: A detail from *December* (plate 140)
ABOVE: A detail from *Nativity* (plate 123)

Flemish Illuminated Manuscripts, 1400–1550

Visitors to art galleries and museums frequently encounter the remarkable and distinctive art of early Netherlandish painting. Almost without exception the works that they see are paintings on panel or canvas executed by the great early exponents of painting in oil – Jan van Eyck, Rogier van der Weyden, Hans Memling, and Hugo van der Goes. Only in exceptional circumstances are the works that they see illuminated manuscripts. Preserved mostly within the great libraries of the world, these handwritten books remain closed on shelves, their painted miniatures, borders, and initials, as well as their calligraphy, inaccessible to all except scholars.

Yet, illuminated manuscripts offer some of the best evidence for our understanding of early Netherlandish painting. In the first place, most of the paintings that they preserve within their pages are a faithful reflection of what the artists sought to create and other contemporary people saw and cherished. In stark contrast to most Netherlandish paintings that survive on panel or canvas, which have been repeatedly repainted, varnished, and cleaned between their creation and the present day, illuminations have rarely been altered by later generations. Kept secure within the binding of a book, the paint of these illuminations is much less vulnerable to damage than that of panels or canvases. Hidden from the fading effect of natural light, painting on the pages of books retains its original colour and clarity of definition. Since manuscripts have also proved less vulnerable to total destruction than independent paintings, the manuscripts that survive provide a better representation of what was originally produced. Large numbers of devotional and liturgical manuscripts offer deep insights into the visual culture of the religious life of both lay and clerical individuals and communities within the century preceding the Reformation. In addition, many manuscripts provide invaluable evidence for an understanding of the development of secular life and culture and the transmutation of the Middle Ages into the early modern period through the Renaissance. The survival of so many Flemish illuminated manuscripts is all the more remarkable given the many religious and political upheavals, as well as the repeated military conflagrations, that have afflicted the region of the southern Low Countries.

Surviving illuminated manuscripts enable us nowadays, whether scholar or lover of art, to track the development of early Netherlandish art through a remarkable period of 150 years. Stretching from 1400 to 1550, the period begins shortly before the advent of the astonishing talent of Jan van Eyck (d. 1441) and ends as Pieter Breugel the Elder (d. 1569) is beginning to paint his masterpieces. Just as in the case of painting on panel and canvas, so painting within books underwent dramatic and decisive transformation within the southern Low Countries. Mirroring, but not merely mimicking,

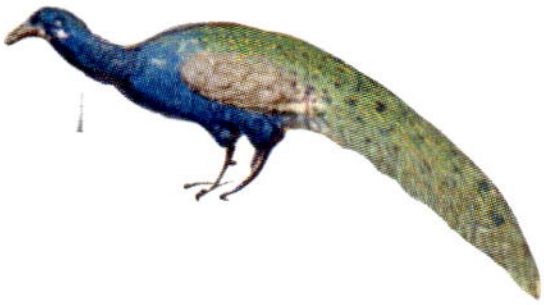

independent painting in their development, illuminated manuscripts at the beginning of the period and those at the end stand worlds apart. Take, for example, the first and last plates in the present volume, the *St Christopher* by the Master of the Beaufort Saints (1) and the miniature of *December* by the renowned Bruges illuminator Simon Bening (140). Sophisticated and accomplished in his art, the painter of the *St Christopher* successfully applied a raw energy of line and application of colour to a traditional subject and the conventions of medieval art. The central image of the saint and its elaborate architectural frame combine to exploit the inherent tension between reality and fictive image and to enhance the spiritual visualisation of the saint by the devout beholder. Bening's mirror of contemporary winter pursuits is dependent on a model created at a date very close to that of this miniature of *St Christopher*. Yet, Bening's imitation of the sophisticated and justifiably famous *Très Riches Heures* of Jean duc de Berry is an artistic challenge – the opportunity for a later artist to emulate a venerable work and seek to transcend it by pushing to the limits his technical expertise and the potential of his medium. Thus Bening's image conjures up both the chill and bare realities of a winter's day and replaces an official record of the owner's residence with a dreamy castle in the sky. Seen from one point of view, Bening's aim was the reverse of that of the Master of the Beaufort Saints. The latter artist sought to enhance the otherworldliness of the holy with touches of immediate reality. Bening, on the other hand, sought to enhance the naturalism of the world that we live in by a subtle application of artifice and idealism.

The present volume illustrates some of the key works created by illuminators working in the towns that now form parts of Belgium and northern France. These illuminators were for the most part commercial or professional artisans who worked for money. Their art was, like that of other medieval art forms, a craft handed down from one generation to another and taught by master to apprentice. Given their setting within one of the most competitively commercial parts of Europe, Flemish illuminators also needed to be fully responsive to their markets. By 1450 the patronage of the Valois dukes of Burgundy and their courtiers supplemented the base market of aristocratic and bourgeois patronage. Renowned for its love of magnificent display and for its conspicuous consumption of material wealth, the Burgundian court did much to shape the development of Flemish illumination. In particular the duke and his court encouraged the production of devotional books that in visual sophistication and splendour equalled and in many cases outdid those produced in any other part of Europe. They also gave renewed impetus to the production of deluxe illustrated manuscripts of secular texts. Much more than Flemish painting on panel or canvas, Flemish illumination was an art of the court. As such it was the natural successor of the refined illumination of Paris that was so closely dependent on the once dominant French royal court.

In addition, Flemish illumination mirrors the developing interest of Flemish painters in the depiction of the natural world – the human form, landscape, and the effects of light. Such interests are particularly evident in the works of the Valenciennes painter and illuminator Simon Marmion. In plates 13–16 and 51–56 we see most vividly Marmion's subtle understanding of how to depict the play of light over forms, structure landscape settings, and use colour to articulate and unify, as well as beautify, a composition. Whereas Marmion rarely repeated his remarkable compositions, other Flemish illuminators devised a wide repertoire of compositional patterns based on the inventions of such early Netherlandish painters as Hugo van der Goes and Justus of Ghent that could be repeatedly exploited without sacrificing the overall quality of a particular book. In this way the Ghent illuminator known as the Master of the First Prayer book of Maximilian generated such high quality masterpieces as the London Hours of William Lord Hastings (37–42). Whereas another Bruges illuminator, the Master of the Dresden Prayer book, illustrated the conventional devotional texts of breviaries and books of hours with images of striking originality (see 69–70, 73–6, 87–8), a contemporary panel painter, Gerard David, translated his compositions into manuscript illuminations (85–6). Another illuminator, the Master of James IV of Scotland, whom some critics have identified as the Ghent painter Gerard Horenbout, largely eschewed the pattern-driven traditions of Flemish manuscript illumination (89–90, 113–4, 120–6). He also applied to illumination a painterly technique and distinctively wide and complex palette. The last of the great Flemish illuminators, Simon Bening, brought the whole story to a close with an astonishing sequence of masterpieces that reveal increasing subtlety in the treatment of sequential narrative and landscape (115–8, 129–32, 134–40).

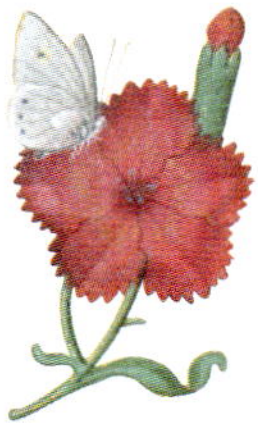

From around the middle of the fifteenth century Flemish illuminators undertook the illustration of a wide range of secular texts. Lacking for the most part a visual tradition on which to draw inspiration, illuminators devised anew numerous narrative cycles. The cycles created by such talented artists as the Créquy Master (7–8), Master of Edward IV (46, 49, 83), Master of the London Wavrin (27, 35, 36, 65–6), Master of the Getty Froissart (63–4) constitute some of the most inventive secular works of the period. By the late 1480s, however, the market for such deluxe secular manuscripts seems to have collapsed. Such late works as those of the Master of the Prayer books of circa 1500 (92–4, 106) are glorious exceptions.

By the late 1470s Flemish illuminators had also begun to experiment with the content of the decorated borders that by convention articulated important divisions of a text and accompanied such pictorial elements as miniatures and historiated initials. Previously two-dimensional in format and decorative in function, these borders began to mirror the naturalism of the pictures that they sat alongside. Most well known among such borders are the so-called scatter or strew flower borders in which flowers, fruit, and insects are depicted as though they had just fallen on the border of imitation gold that surrounds either text or image. Frequently reproduced in modern times, these flower borders are widely regarded as the quintessential element of Flemish illuminated manuscripts. Other less well-known types of border that exploited similar conceits are those that depict fantastic architectural structures (97, 98). Yet others seek to suggest that it is the text, not the illumination that is closest to the viewer.

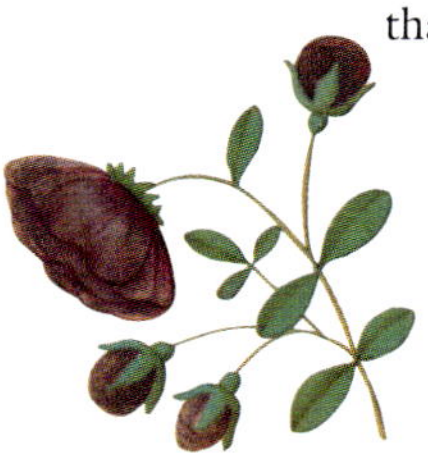

They play with the illusion that the illumination continues across the whole page, linking each of the four sides of the border, and passing underneath the text (115). In other manuscripts borders appear to continue the subject of a miniature, but do so in such a way that the miniature resembles a zoom-in detail from the full-page image, the outline of which is suggested by the borders (103, 116).

Flemish illuminated manuscripts were created for an international market and not merely for local consumption. They were sought after by people who lived far beyond the confines of the Low Countries, in both southern and northern Europe. As exemplified by the first three works illustrated in the present volume (1–3), English patronage of Flemish manuscripts took root early on. Subsequently, close political, dynastic, and cultural links between England and Flanders during the reign of Edward IV enabled the English king to acquire many of the Flemish manuscripts that have survived from the Old Royal Library (45–50, 61–6). The taste for Flemish manuscripts also extended to Italy, Spain, Portugal, Germany, France, and Scotland. Around the time of the important double marriage that bound the Habsburg heirs of the dukes of Burgundy to the ascendant stars of the royal houses of Castile and Aragon, both Queen Isabella of Castile and her daughter Joanna came to own luxurious Flemish manuscripts of devotional texts (85–90, 97–100). Some time during their residence in the Low Countries an Italian merchant and his wife had totally revamped by Flemish illuminators an earlier Italian book of hours (101–2). In the 1530s, the Portuguese prince Dom Fernando commissioned an illuminated genealogy from the Bruges illuminator

Simon Bening (134–6). While a Portuguese artist was entrusted to draw the compositions for the genealogy, no expense was spared in transporting these drawings from Lisbon to Bruges. For illumination none in Europe was more accomplished than the artists of the southern Netherlands.

The reproductions in this book are all taken from Flemish illuminated manuscripts that now form part of the vast collections of the British Library. These manuscripts have been acquired for the British nation over the past 250 years by purchase and gift. A large number, like those made for Edward IV (45–50, 61–6), Henry VII (91, 92, 94, 106), and Henry VIII (111, 133), have remained in Britain from shortly after their production. Others passed into the great collections of Sir Robert Cotton (10, 20, 30, 35), Robert and Edward Harley, successive Earls of Oxford (4, 7, 9, 11, 25–6, 29, 59–60), and Sir Hans Sloane, Bt. (2) all of which came to form the foundations of the British Museum in 1753. Such landmarks of Flemish manuscript illumination as the so-called Hours of Philip the Fair (73–76), the Breviary of Isabella of Castile (85–90), the Hours of Joanna of Castile (97–100), the Golf Book (129–32), the Genealogy of Dom Fernando of Portugal (134–6) and calendar leaves by Simon Bening (137–40) became national property in the following century. Together with the acquisition of other less prominent Flemish manuscripts (8, 23, 31, 34, 44, 57, 58, 71–2, 77, 81, 101–2, 107–10, 115–6, 127–8), they reflect both the shrewd discernment of the mid-nineteenth-century custodian of the national collection of manuscripts, Sir Frederic Madden, and the beginnings of British interest in the study of early Netherlandish painting. Other key works, such as the London Hours of William Lord Hastings (37–42), the Huth Hours (51–56), and the Hours of Bona Sforza (120–6) followed in their footsteps over the past one hundred years. Together with two manuscripts from the collection of Baron Ferdinand de Rothschild (95–6, 113–4) and three from the collection of Henry Yates Thompson (12, 17, 82), they constitute some of the most outstanding gifts of manuscripts made to British nation.

The 140 colour plates contained in the present volume are arranged broadly in the order that the works that they reproduce were made, starting at around 1400 and ending shortly before 1550. The captions that accompany the plates provide the subject of the illumination reproduced as well as the title or text of the manuscript in which that illumination appears. In addition they offer attributions to a particular artist or artistic grouping, and assign a place of origin and date. The measurements (in millimetres) provide the dimensions of the page on which the illumination appears. Where possible, the page is reproduced at actual size. At the end of the caption is the full British Library manuscript reference.

In many cases one reproduction must represent a manuscript that contains fifty or more miniatures. Selecting from such a rich store is both an invidious and a laborious task. It is, however, also a joy. Just as I have gained much pleasure from making this selection, so, I hope, those who cast their eyes over the following pages will come to appreciate something of the beauty of the works created by Flemish manuscript illuminators.

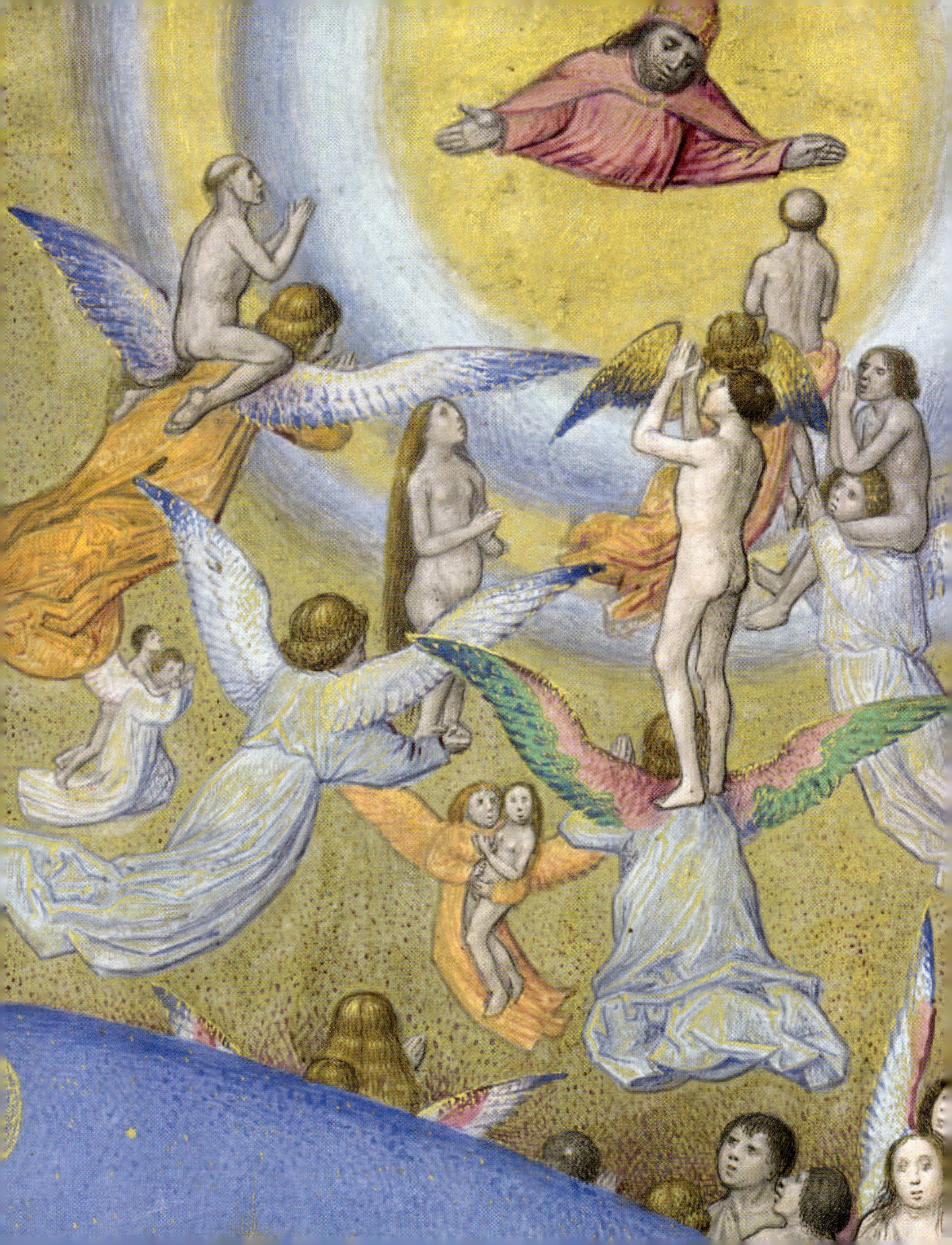

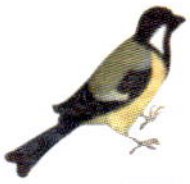

THE PLATES

OPPOSITE: A detail from *Souls of the blessed arriving in Heaven* (plate 41)

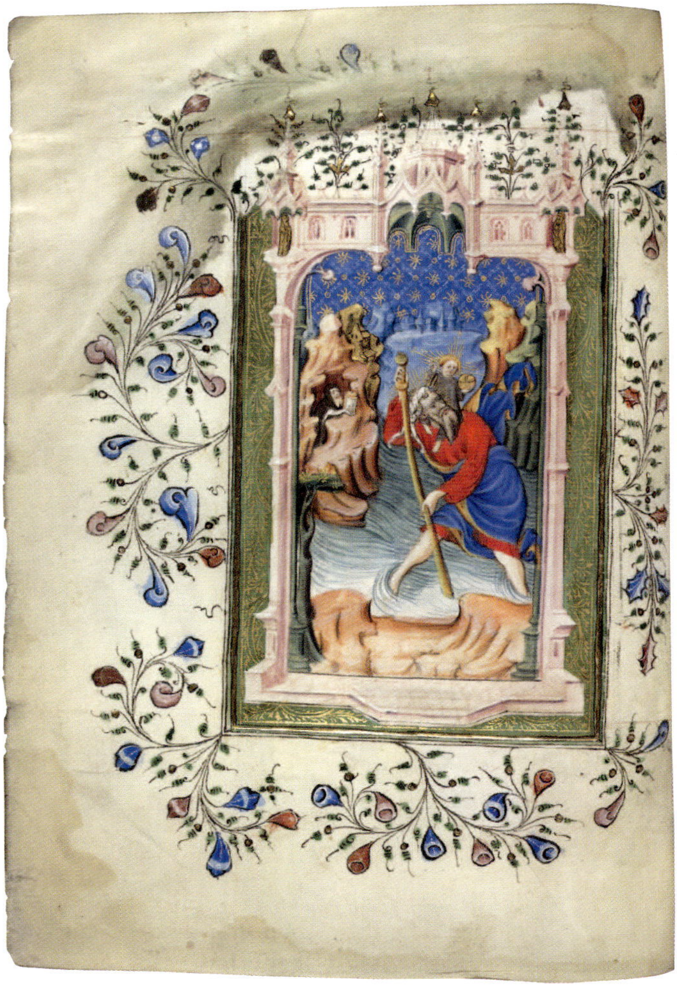

1 *St Christopher*
Psalter-Hours
Master of the Beaufort Saints
Bruges, early 15th century
215 × 150 mm
Royal MS 2 A xviii, f. 11v

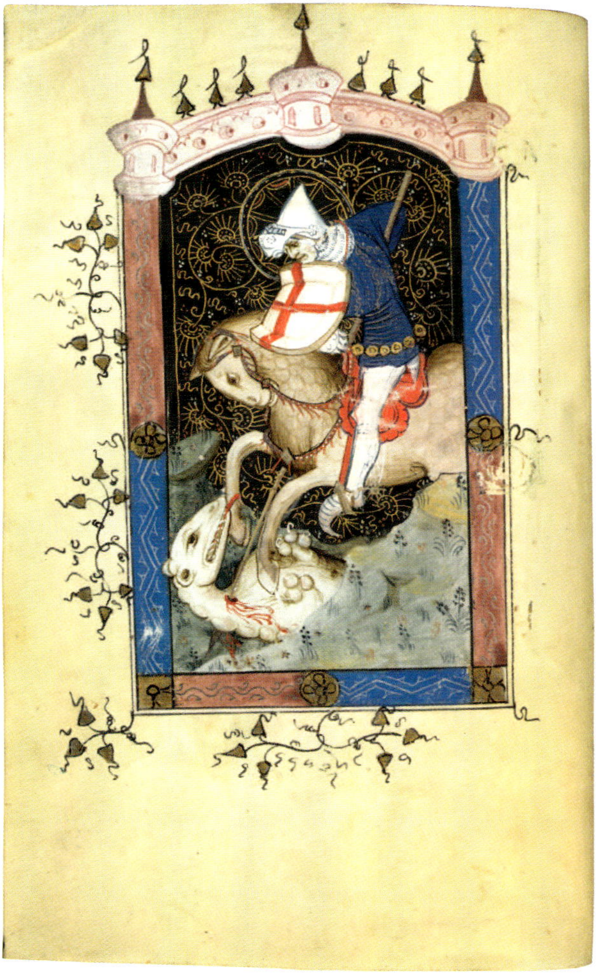

2 *St George*
Book of Hours, use of Sarum
Pink Canopies Group
Bruges, *c.* 1390–1400
197 × 123 mm
Sloane MS 2683, f. 14v

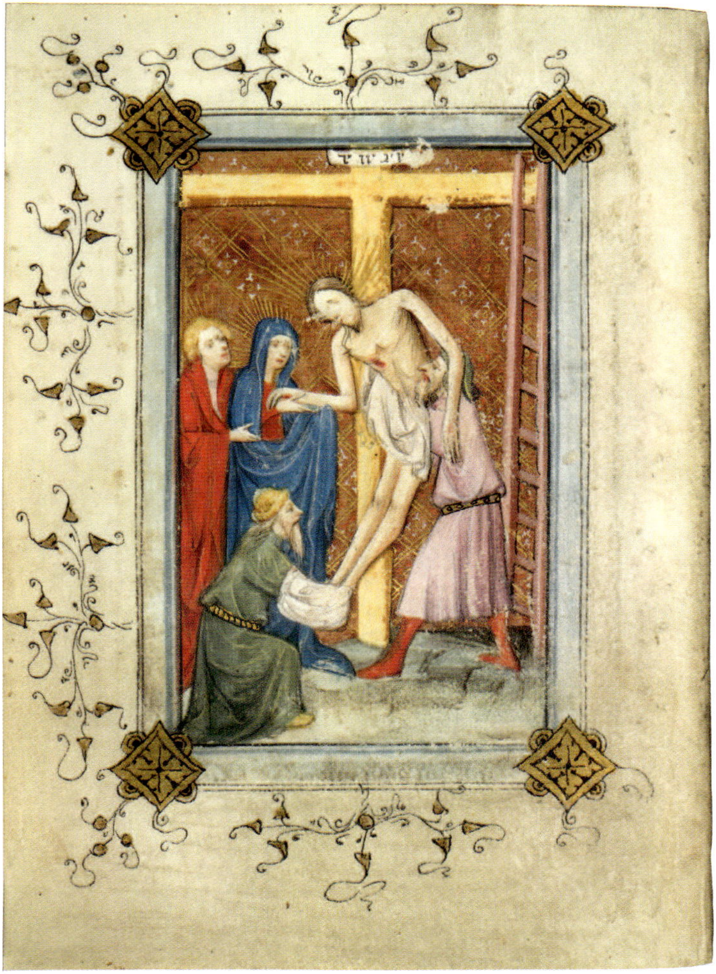

3 Descent from the Cross
Book of Hours, use of Sarum
Bruges, *c.* 1410
190 × 140 mm
Add. MS 27948, f. 33v

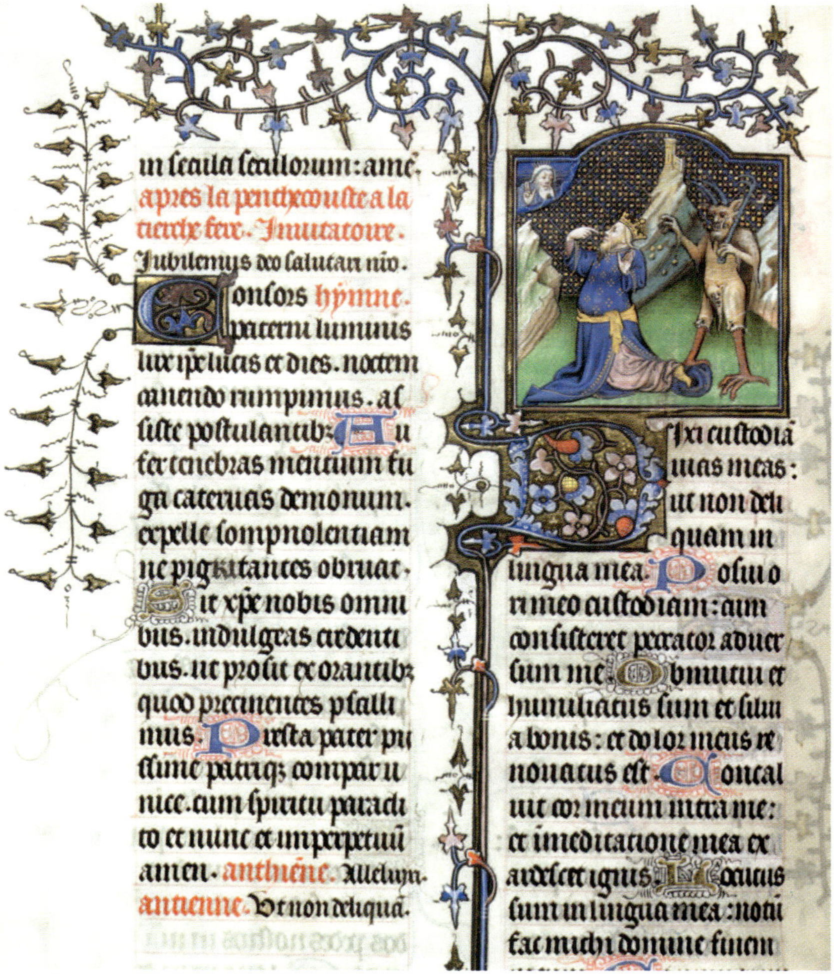

4 *David and the Devil*
Breviary of John the Fearless
Master of Guillebert de Mets
Paris, between 1413 and 1419
250 × 132 mm
Harley MS 2897, f. 33v (detail)

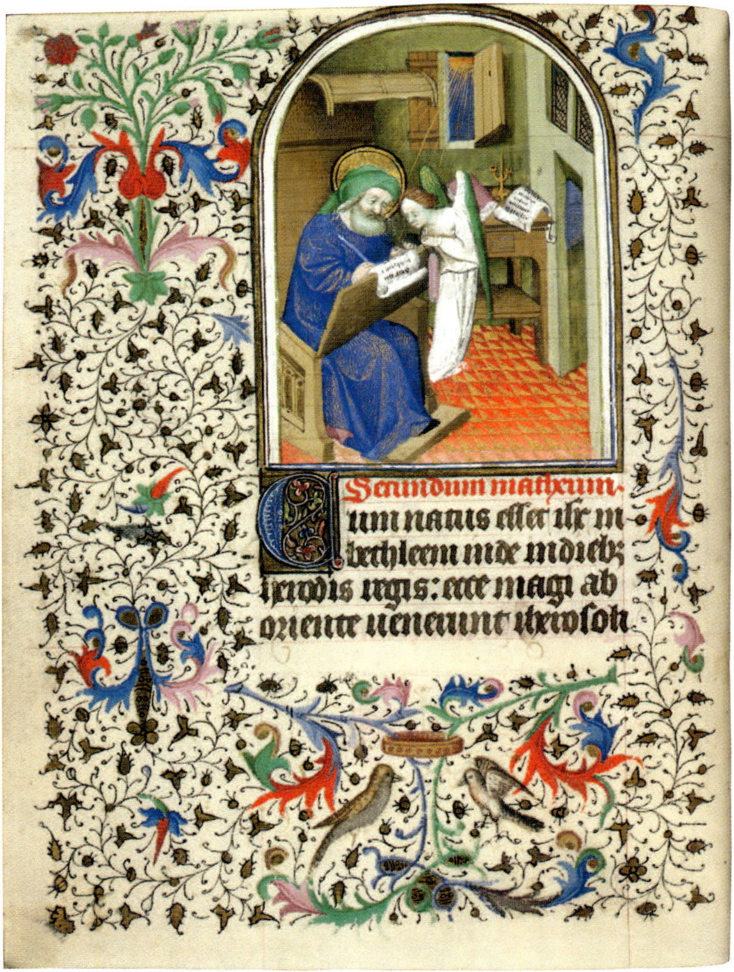

5 *St Matthew in his study*
Book of Hours, use of Amiens
Master of Raoul d'Ailly
Amiens, *c.* 1430–1440
175 × 133 mm
Add. MS 31835, f. 16v

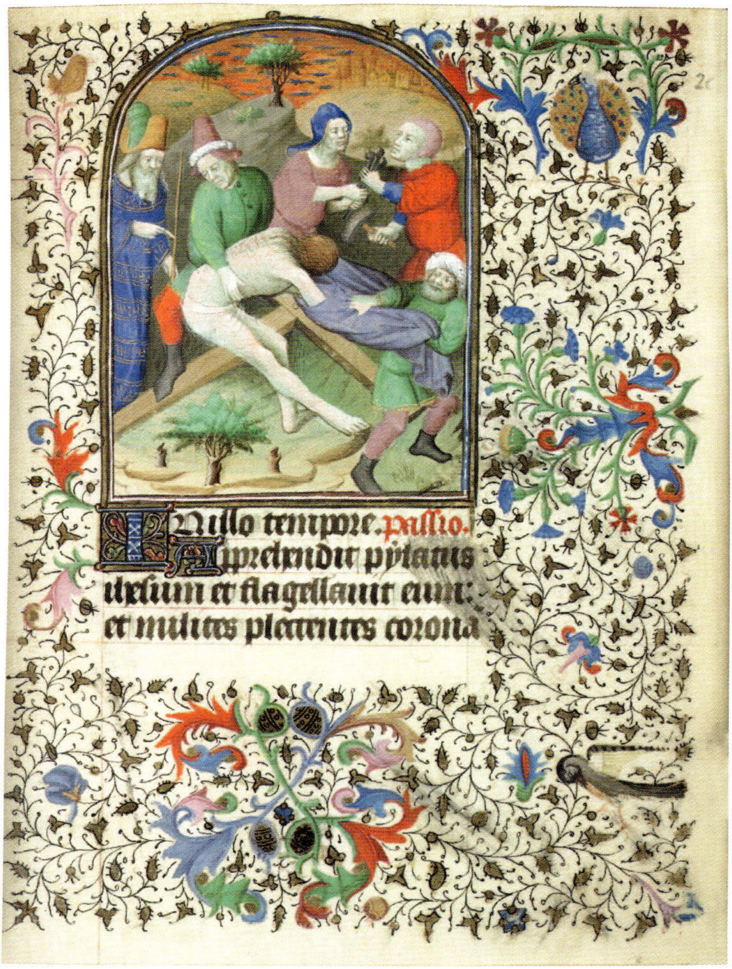

6 Derobing of Christ
Book of Hours, use of Amiens
Associate of the Master of Raoul d'Ailly
Amiens, c. 1430–1440
175 × 133 mm
Add. MS 31835, f. 20

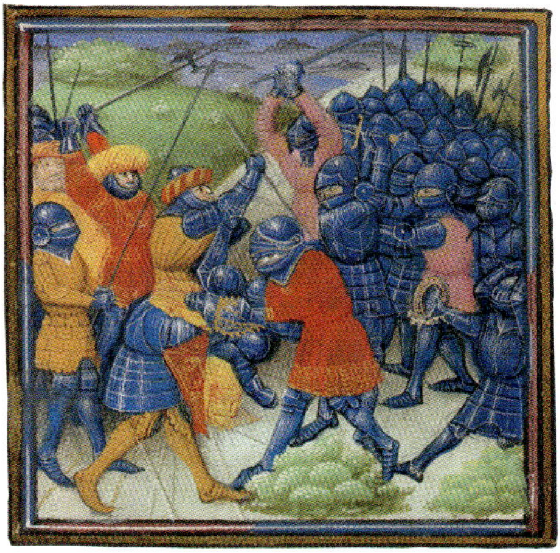

7 *Christians fighting Saracens*
Roman de Mélusine. Made for Jean de Créquy, lord of Fressin and Canaples
Créquy Master
Amiens, *c*. 1450
330 × 235 mm
Harley MS 4418, f. 99 (detail shown actual size)

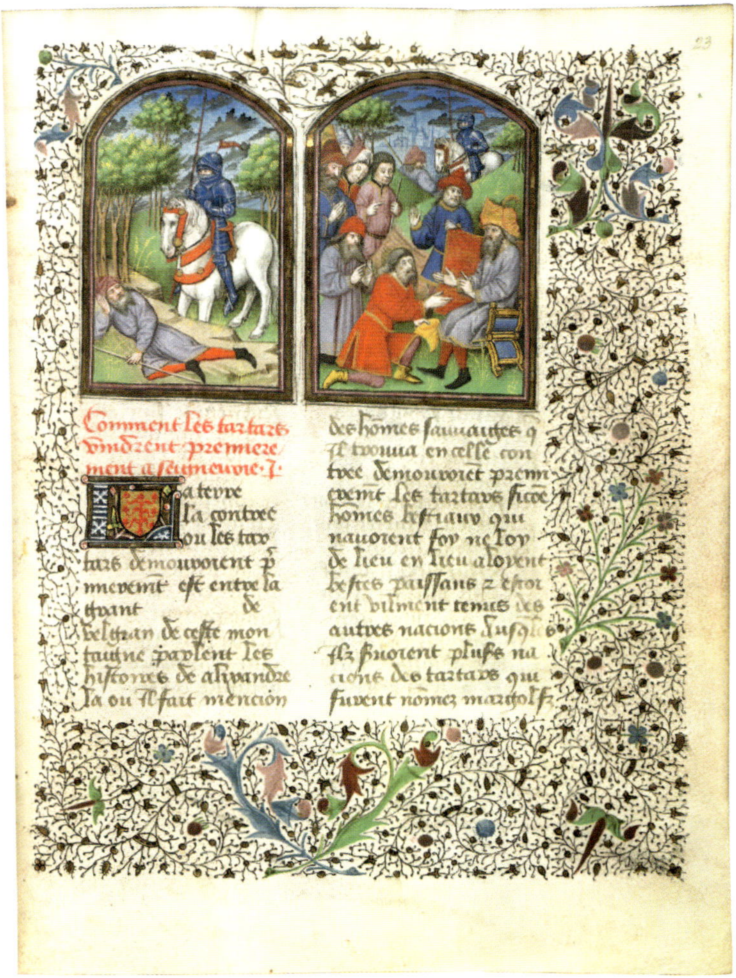

8 *The Dream of Cangnis* and *The Tartars paying homage to Cangnis*
Jean Hayton, *Fleur des histoires de la terre d'Orient*.
Made for Jean de Créquy, lord of Fressin and Canaples
Créquy Master, Amiens, *c*. 1450
285 × 205 mm
Add. MS 17971, f. 23

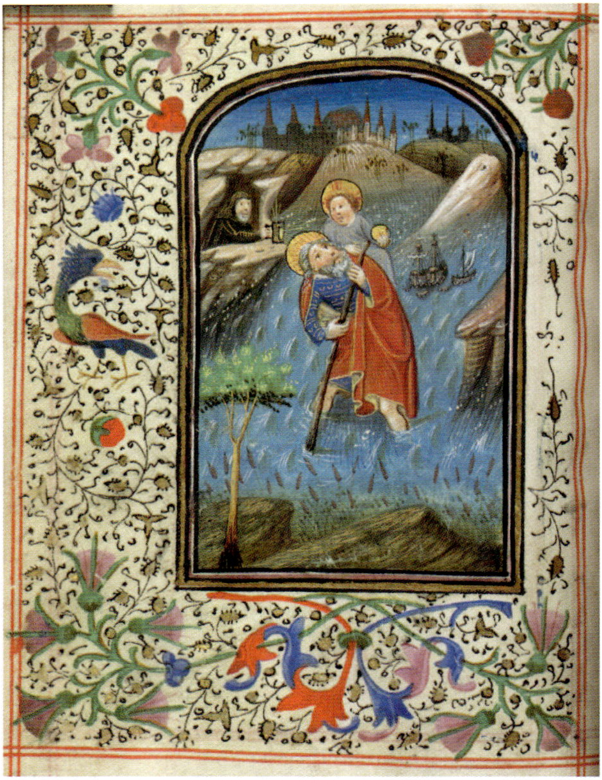

9 *St Christopher*
Book of Hours, use of Sarum
Gold Scrolls Group
Flanders, *c.* 1440–1450
112 × 85 mm
Harley MS 2846, f. 38v (actual size)

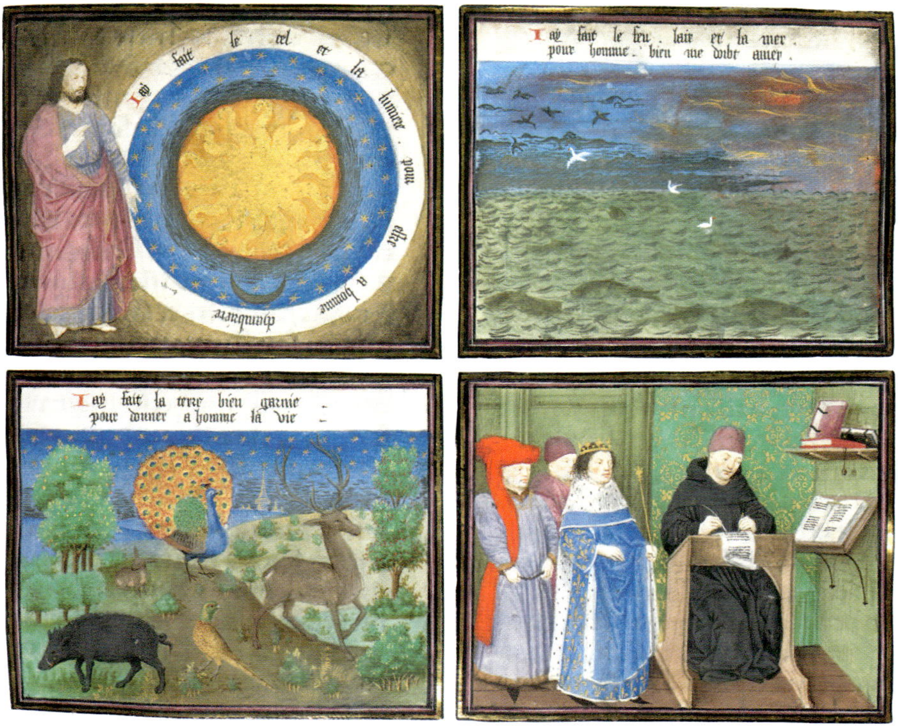

10 *The Creation of the elements; the translator and Charles V of France*
Bartholomaeus Anglicus, *De proprietatibus rerum*. French translation by Jean Corbechon. Made for Jean de Créquy, lord of Fressin and Canaples
Master of the *Annunciation* of the Rambures Hours, Amiens, *c.* 1450
455 × 330 mm
Cotton MS Augustus A vi, f. 11 (detail)

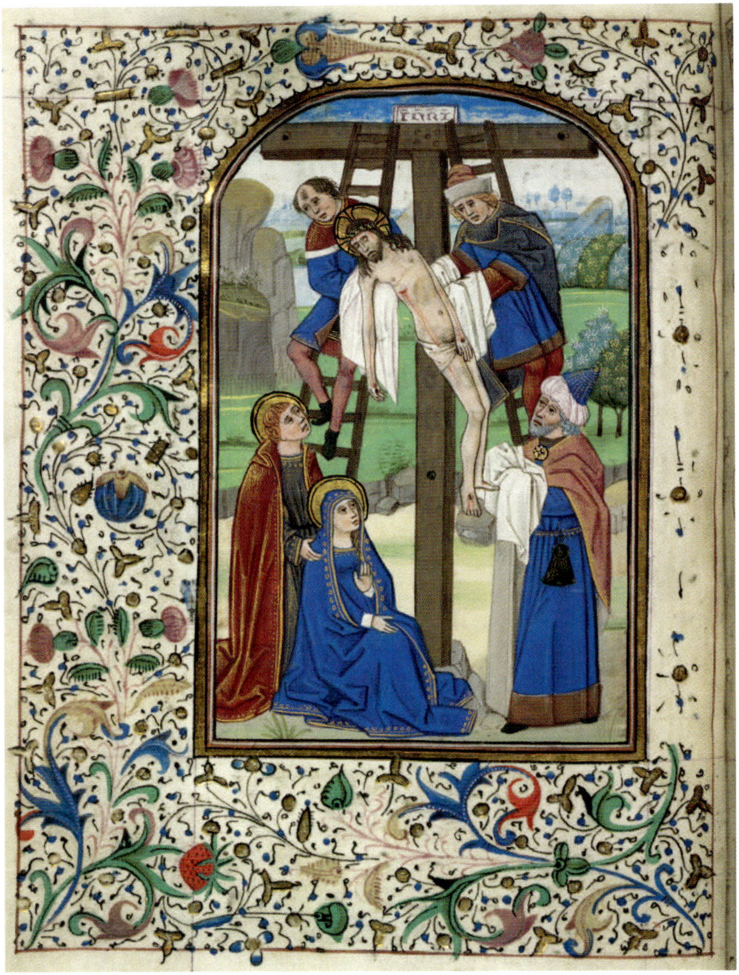

11 *Descent from the Cross*
Book of Hours, use of the Collegiate Church of St Hermes, Ronse
Master of the Polemical Texts
Bruges, c. 1465
187 × 135 mm
Harley MS 1211, f. 16v

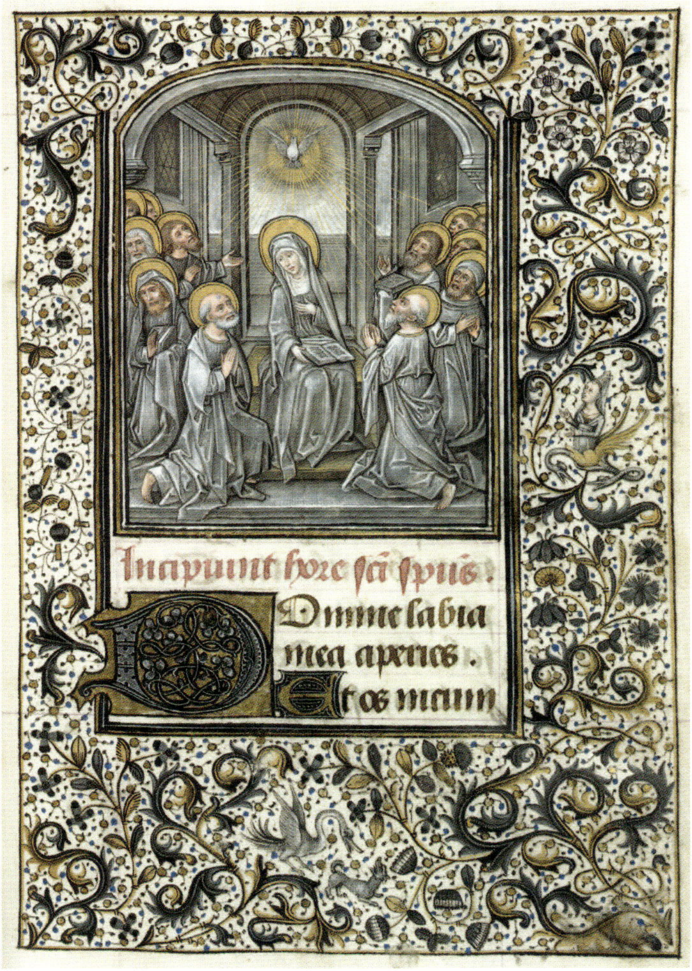

12 *Descent of the Holy Spirit*
Hours of Jacques de Brégilles (d. 1475)
Willem Vrelant
Bruges, 1460s
190 × 130 mm
Yates Thompson MS 4, f. 35

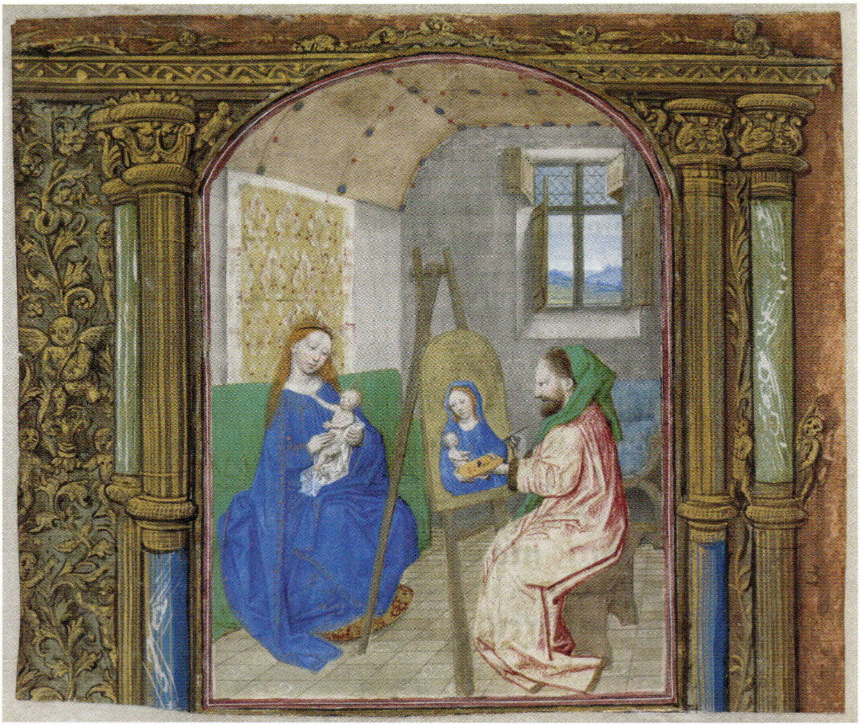

13 *St Luke painting the Virgin and Child*
Leaf from the so-called Hours of Ladislas IV Vasa
Simon Marmion
Valenciennes, 1460s
117 × 133 mm (upper portion)
Add. MS 71117, f. B (detail)

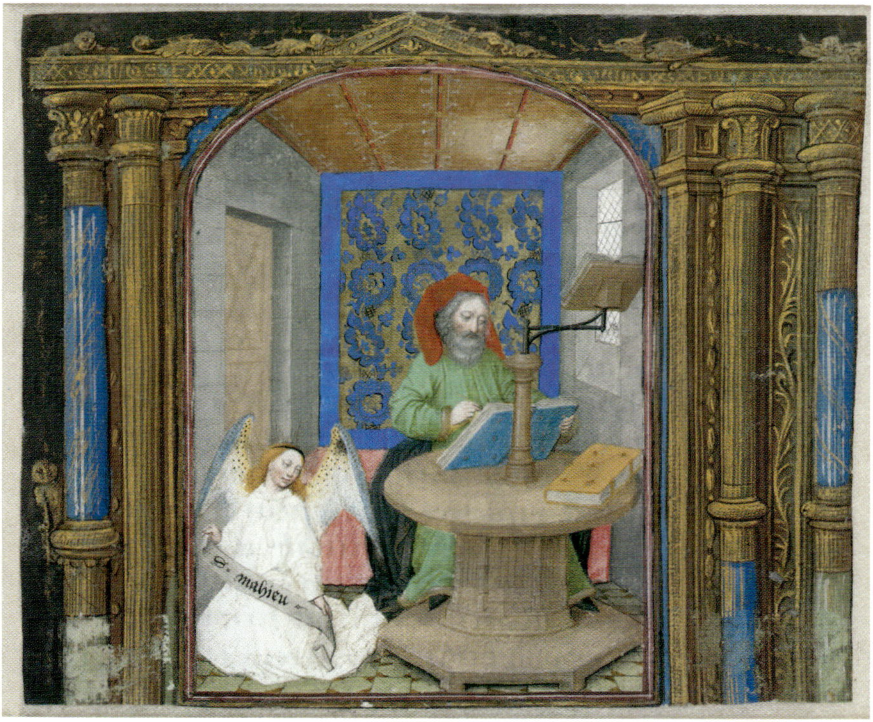

14 *St Matthew in his study*
Leaf from the so-called Hours of Ladislas IV Vasa
Simon Marmion
Valenciennes, 1460s
117 × 135 mm (upper portion)
Add. MS 71117, f. C (detail)

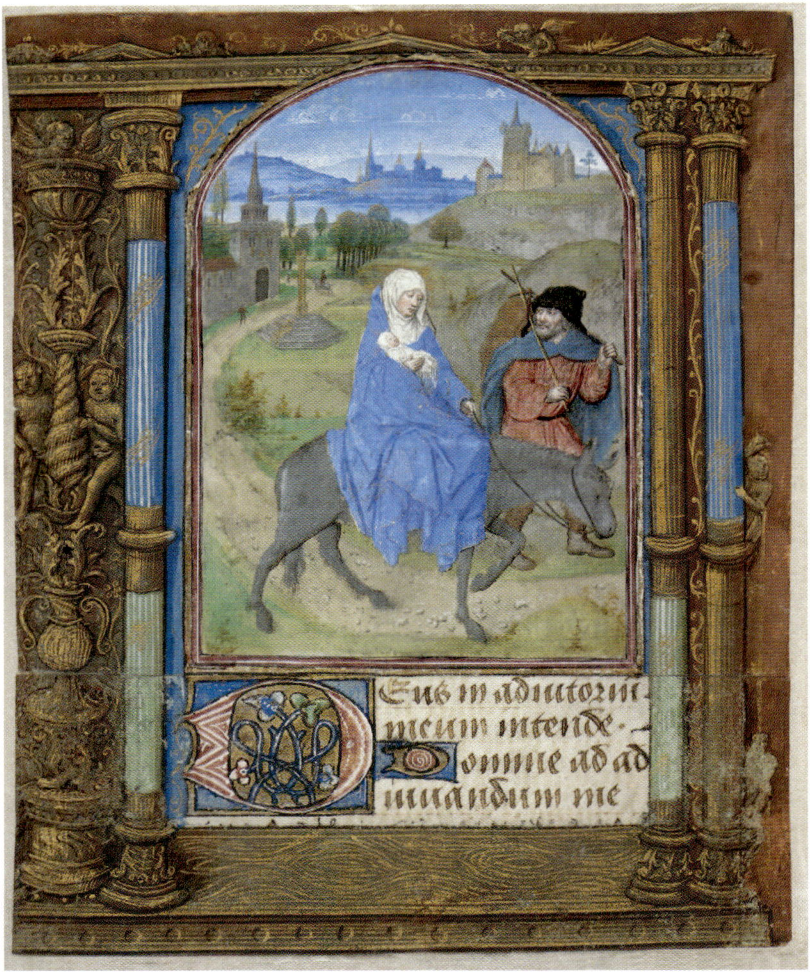

15 *Flight into Egypt*
Leaf from the so-called Hours of Ladislas IV Vasa
Simon Marmion
Valenciennes, 1460s
165 × 130 mm
Add. MS 71117, f. G

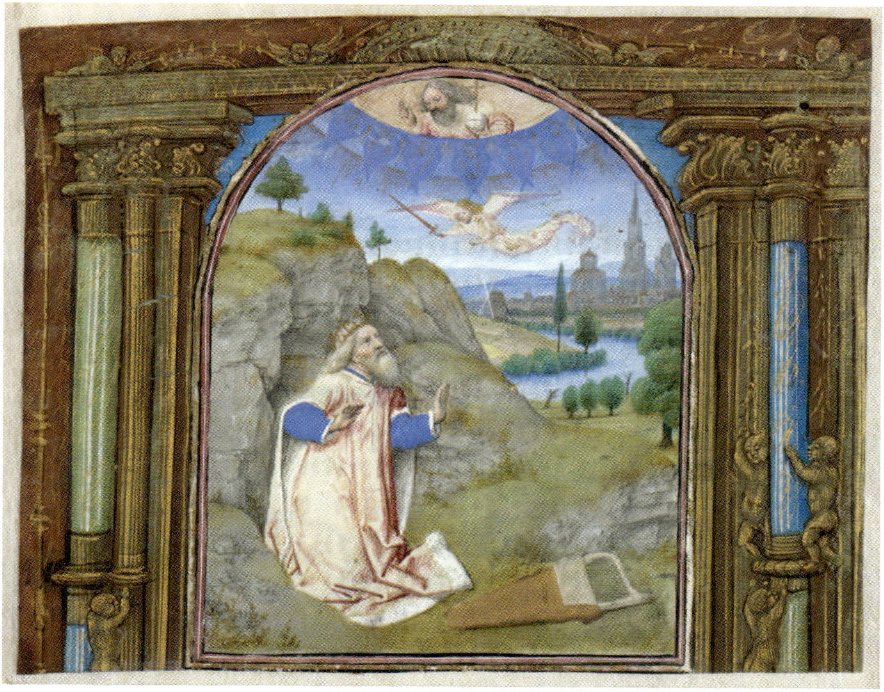

16 David in prayer
Leaf from the so-called Hours of Ladislas IV Vasa
Simon Marmion
Valenciennes, 1460s
105 × 130 mm
Add. MS 71117, f. J

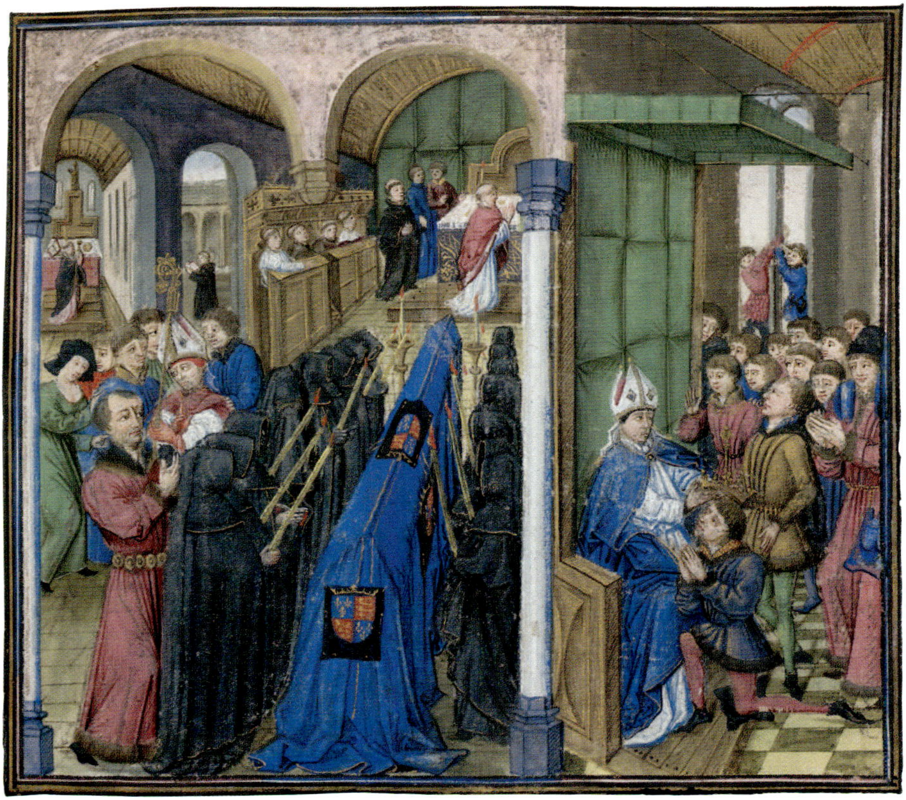

17 *Funeral of William the Conqueror and Coronation of William Rufus*
Grande Chronique de Normandie. Made for Philippe de Crèvecoeur, lord of Les Querdes
Follower of the Girart Master
Brussels, *c*. 1465–1468
360 × 260 mm
Yates Thompson MS 33, f. 176 (detail)

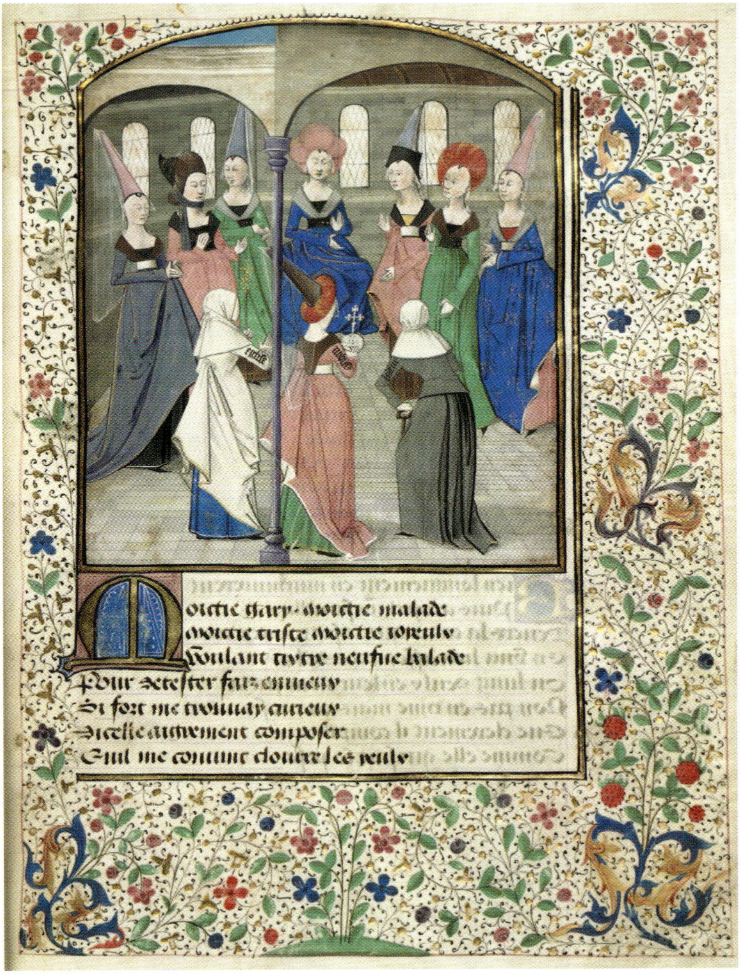

18 *The Three Estates (Church, Nobles and Labour) in debate before Theology, Logic, Arithmetic, Geometry and Music*
Charles Soillot, *Débat de félicité*
Master of the *Hiéron*, Bruges, between 1464 and 1467
350 × 260 mm
Arundel MS 71, f. 24

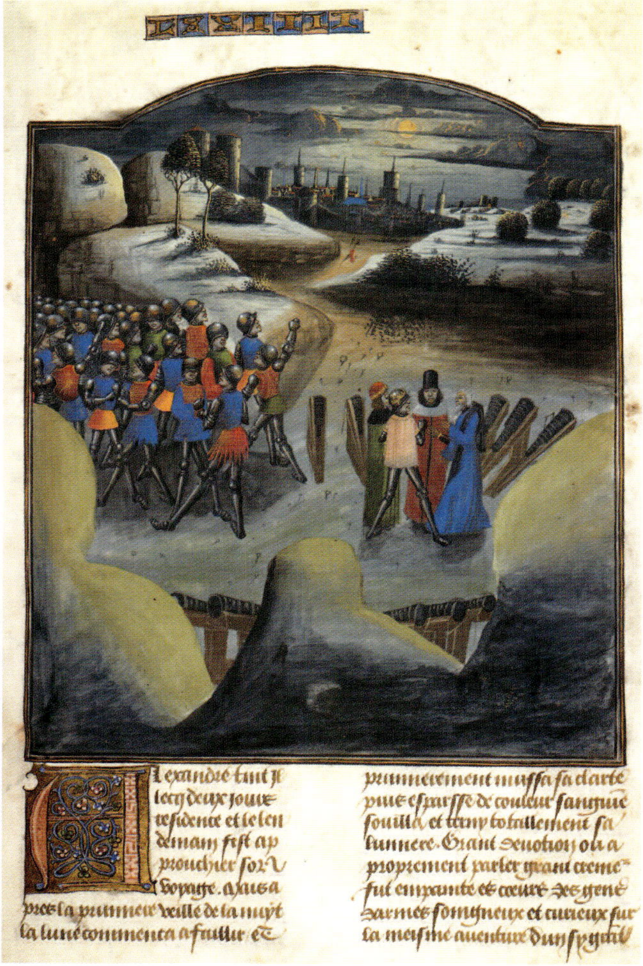

19 *Alexander the Great consulting his astrologers about an eclipse of the sun after the battle of Arbela*
Quintus Curtius Rufus, *Historia Alexandri magni*. French translation by Vasco da Lucena.
First owned by the Hospitaller knight Philippe de Cluys
Master of the Vienna *Chroniques d'Angleterre*, Bruges, between 1468 and 1475
430 × 315 mm
Burney MS 169, f. 69

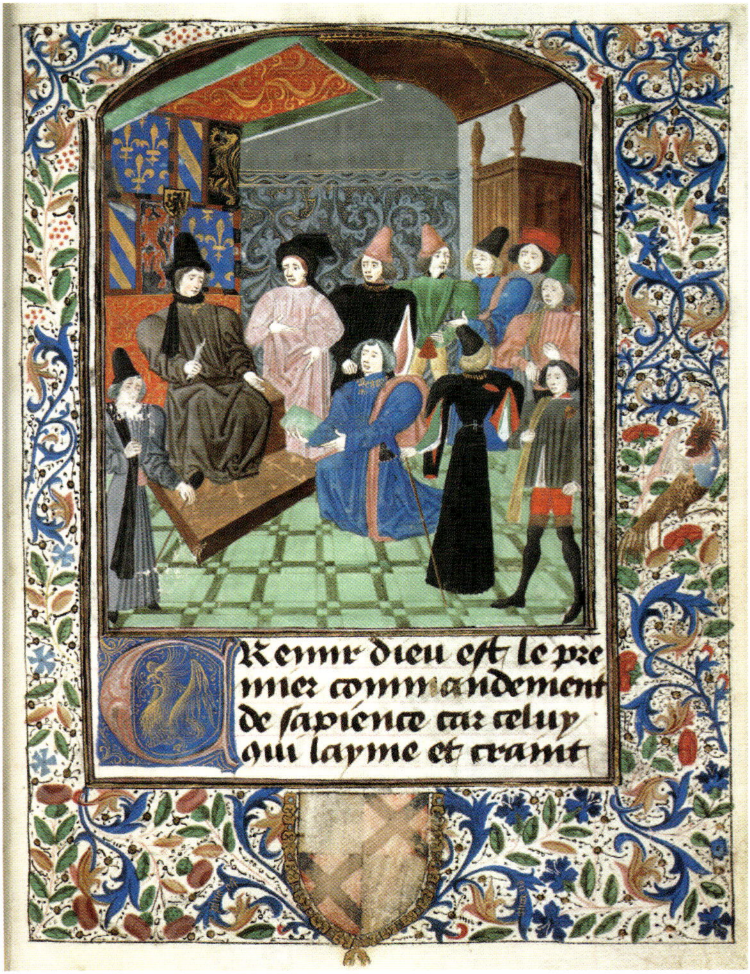

20 *Gilbert de Lannoy presenting his book to Philip the Good, Duke of Burgundy*
Gilbert de Lannoy, *L'Instruction d'un jeune prince*. Made for Louis of Gruuthuse
Master of the Harley Froissart
Bruges, *c.* 1465–1470
257 × 178 mm
Cotton MS Vespasian B i, f. 15

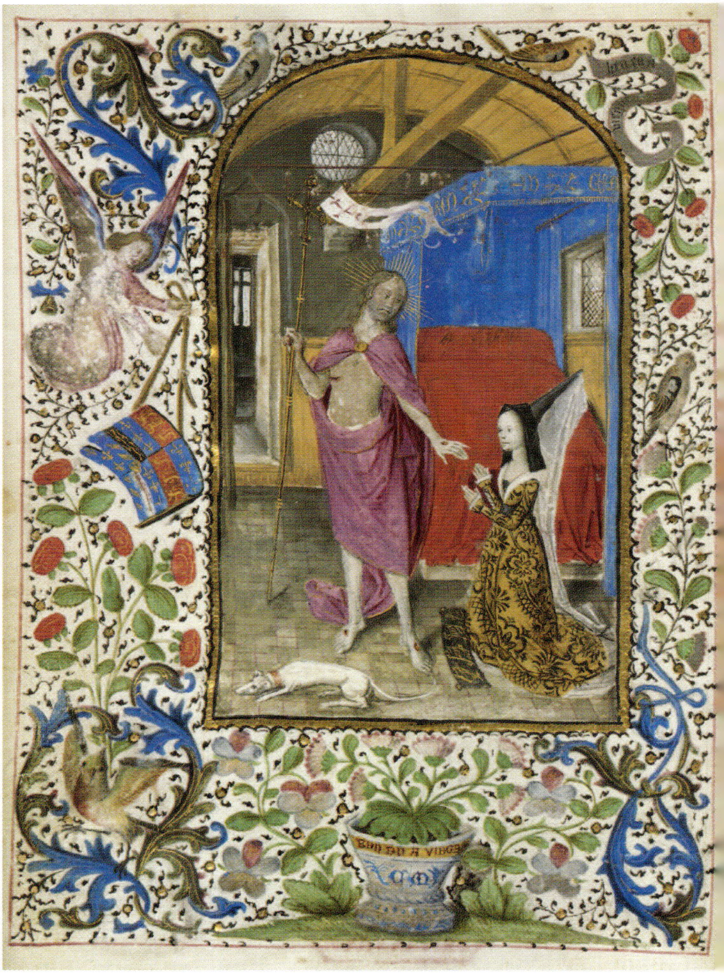

21 & 22 *Margaret of York and the risen Christ*
Nicolas Finet, *Dialogue de la duchesse de Bourgogne à Jésus Christ*.
Made for Margaret of York, Duchess of Burgundy
Follower of the Girart Master, Brussels, shortly after 1468
200 × 140 mm
Add. MS 7970, ff. IV-2

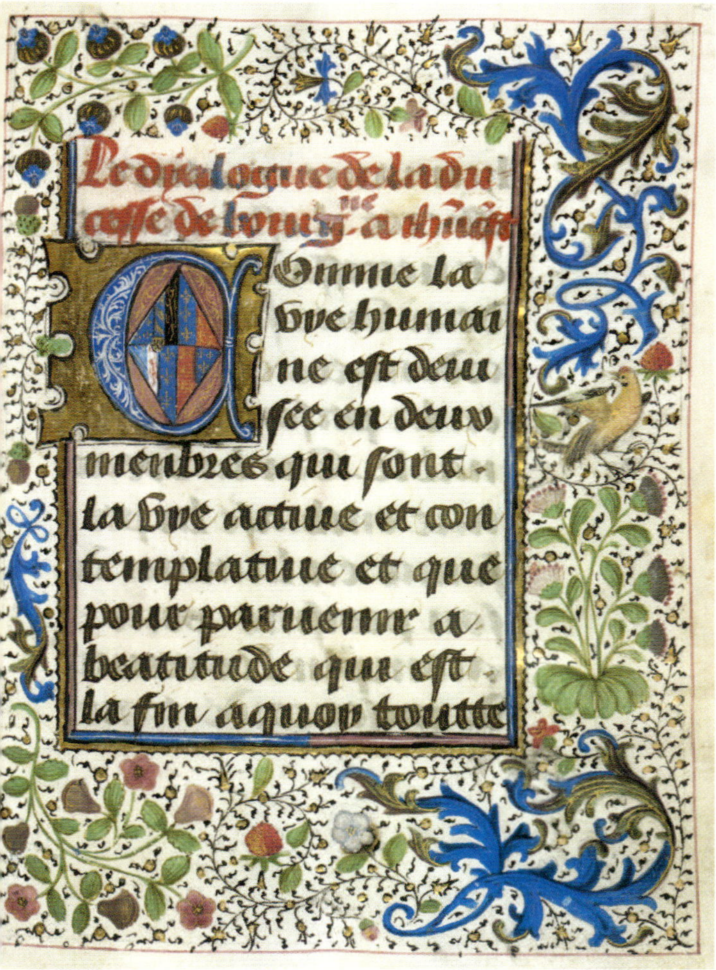
Le dyalogue dela du
ne
cesse de bourg a ihucrist
Comme la
vye humai
ne est deu
see en deux
membres qui sont .
la vye actiue et con
templatiue et que
pour paruenir a
beatitude qui est
la fin aquoy toutte

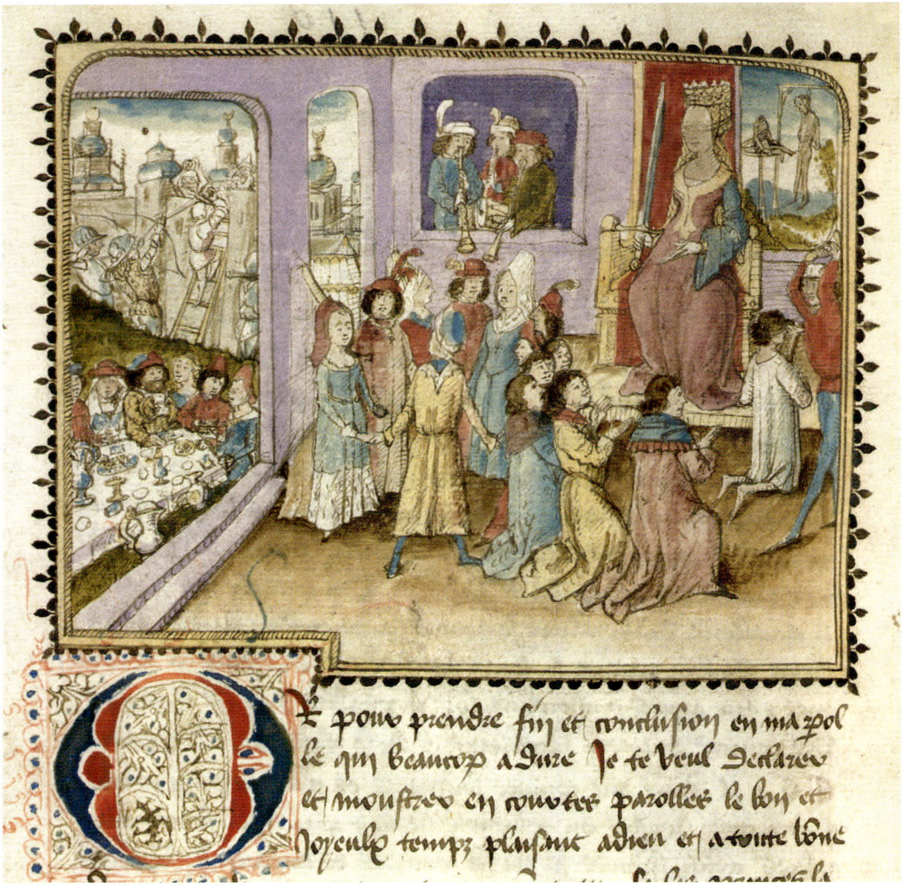

23 *The Rule of Justice*
Jean de Lannoy (?), *L'Imaginacion de la vraye noblesse.*
Lille (?), c. 1470–1475
285 × 205 mm
Add. MS 15469, f. 73v (detail)

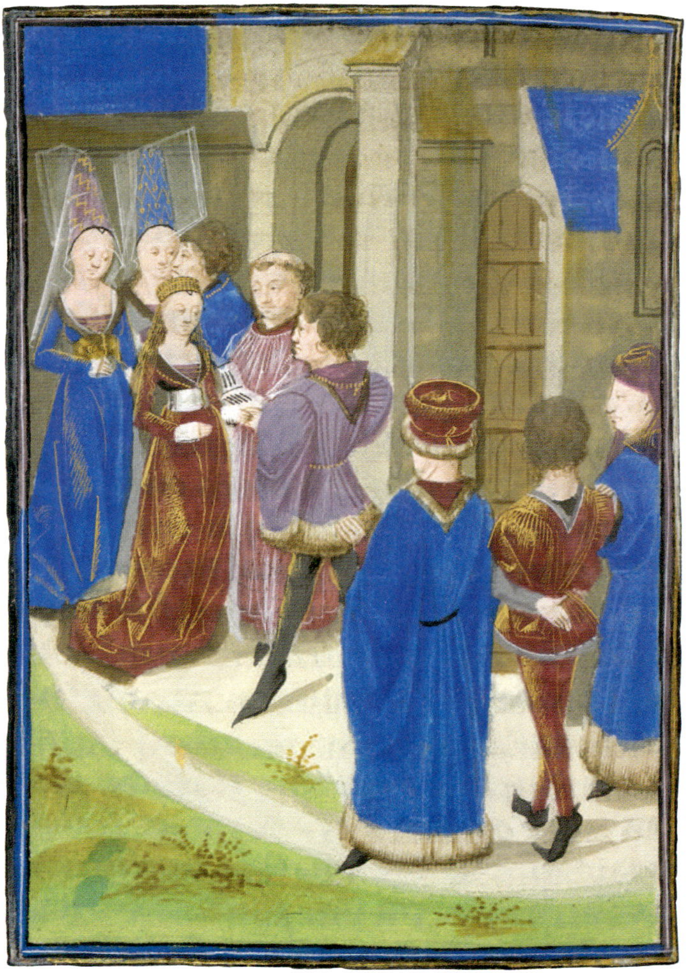

24 *Marriage*
Valerius Maximus, *Facta et Dicta Memorabilia*. French translation by
Simon de Hesdin and Nicolas de Gonesse
Rambures Master, Bruges (?), c. 1470
490 × 348 mm
Royal MS 17 F iv, f. 65v (detail)

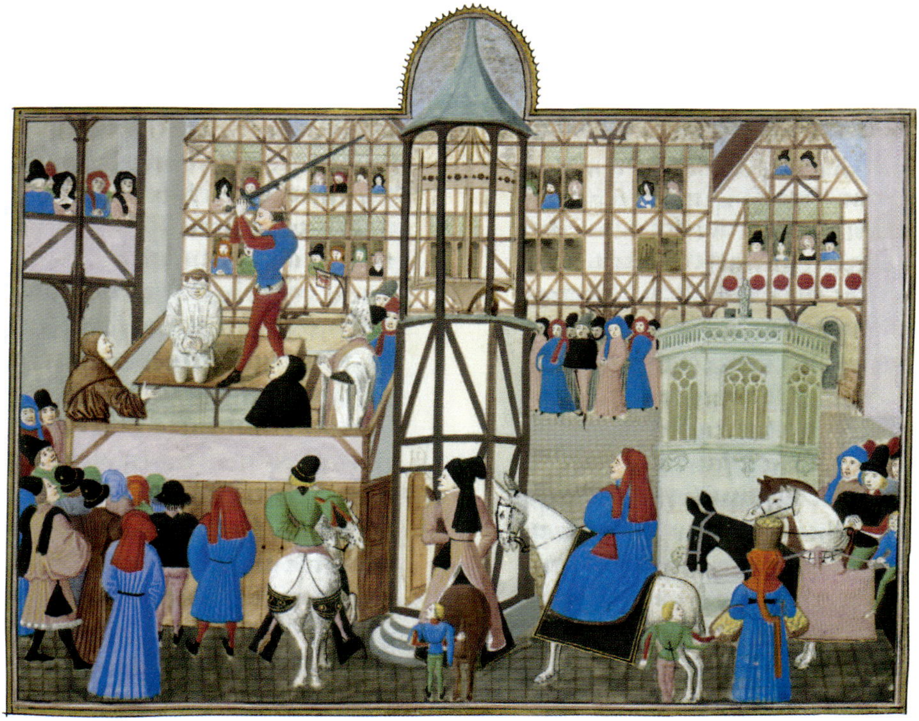

25 *Execution of Amerigot Marcel*
Jean Froissart, *Chroniques*, vol. 4. Made for Philippe de Comines, lord of Argenton
Master of the Harley Froissart
Bruges, c. 1472–1473
420 × 320 mm
Harley MS 4379, f. 64 (detail)

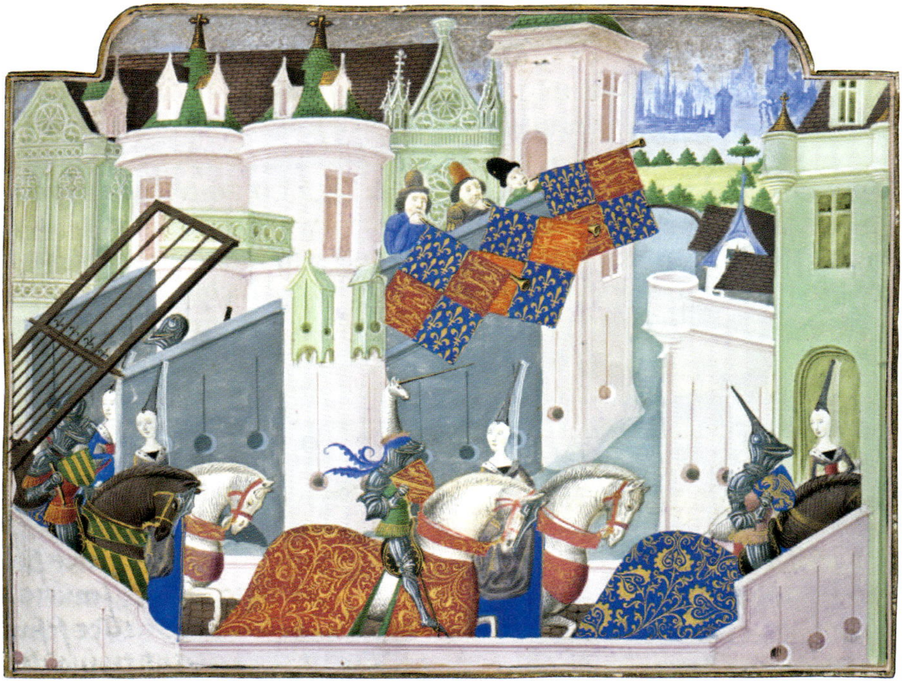

26 *Knights and ladies riding to London tournament*
Jean Froissart, *Chroniques*, vol. 4. Made for Philippe de Comines, lord of Argenton
Master of the Harley Froissart
Bruges, c. 1472–1473
420 × 320 mm
Harley MS 4379, f. 99 (detail)

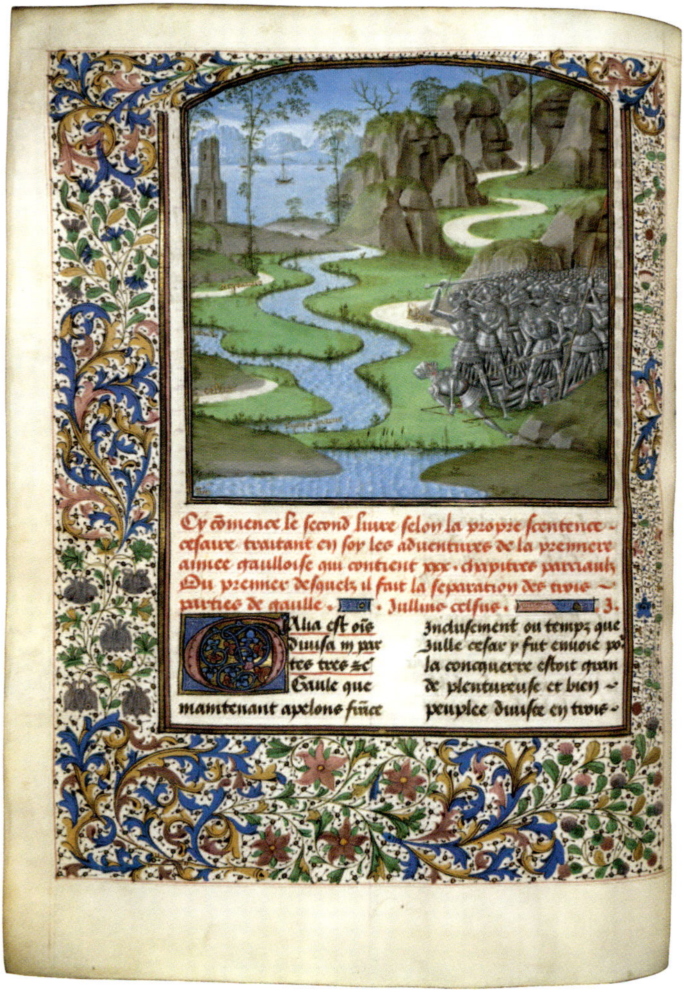

27 *View of Gaul*
Julius Caesar, *Commentarii*. French translation attributed to Jan du Quesne
Master of the London Wavrin
Bruges, between 1473 and 1476
400 × 290 mm
Royal MS 16 G viii, f. 86v

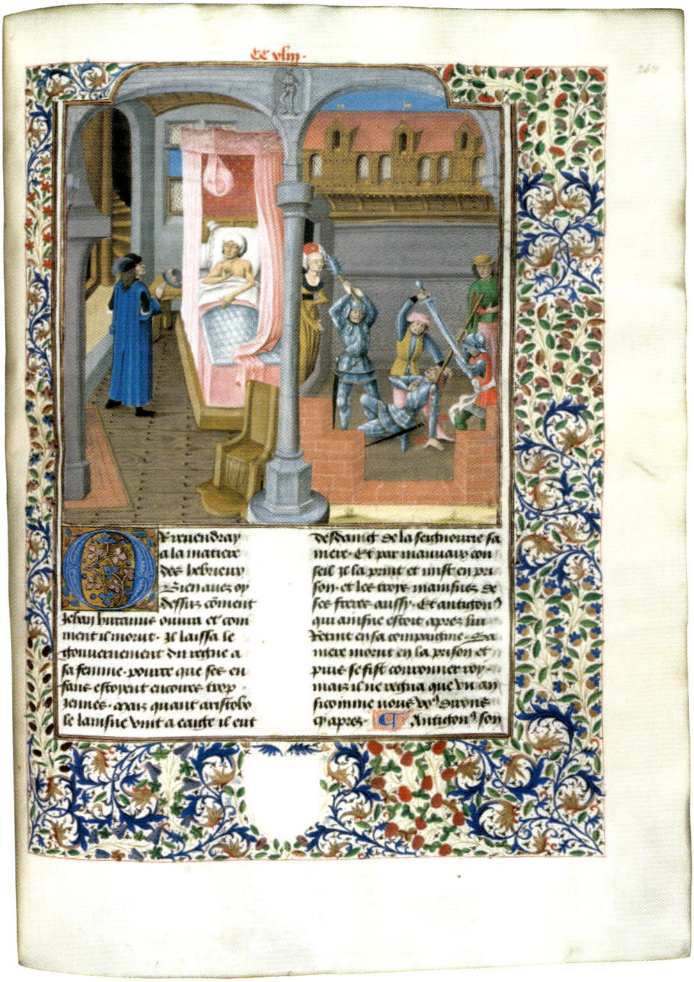

28 *Death of Aristobulus and murder of Antigonus*
L'Histoire tripartite
Master of the Soane Josephus
Bruges, between 1473 and 1480
467 × 340 mm
Royal MS 18 E v, f. 263

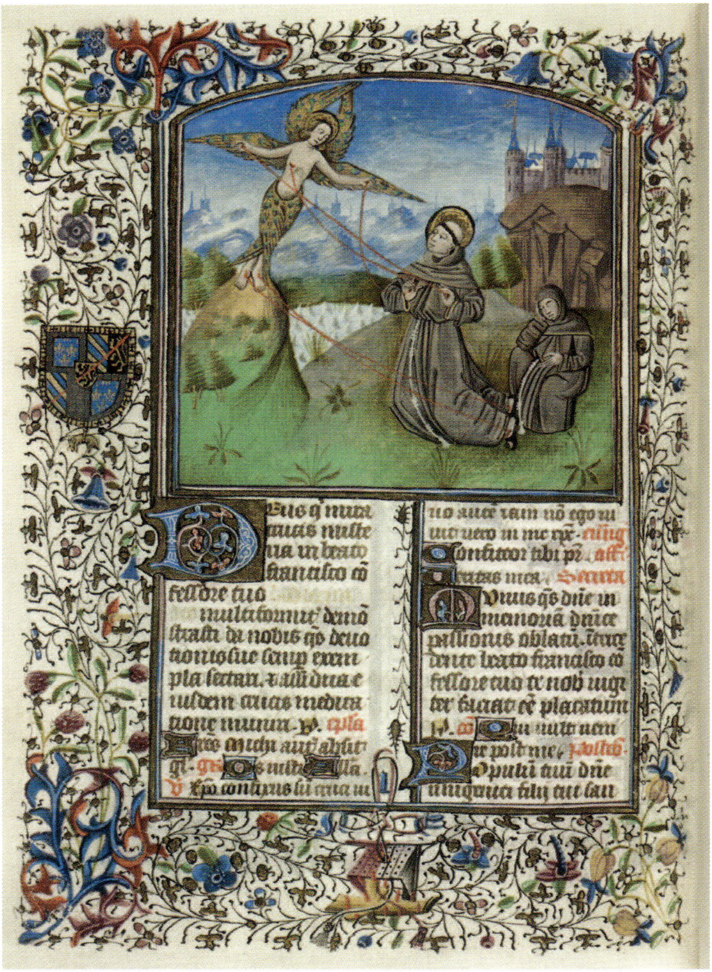

29 *St Francis receiving the stigmata*
Breviary of Anthony of Burgundy
Workshop of Jacques Pilavaine (?)
Mons, c. 1475
210 × 145 mm
Harley MS 2967, f. 214v

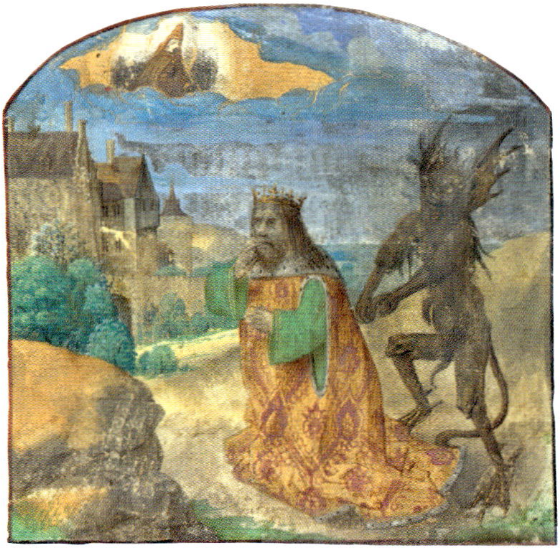

30 David and the Devil
A leaf from the Breviary of Margaret of York, Duchess of Burgundy
Vienna Master of Mary of Burgundy
Ghent, *c.* 1475–1480
243 × 176 mm
Cotton MS Tiberius A ii, f. 1 (detail, actual size)

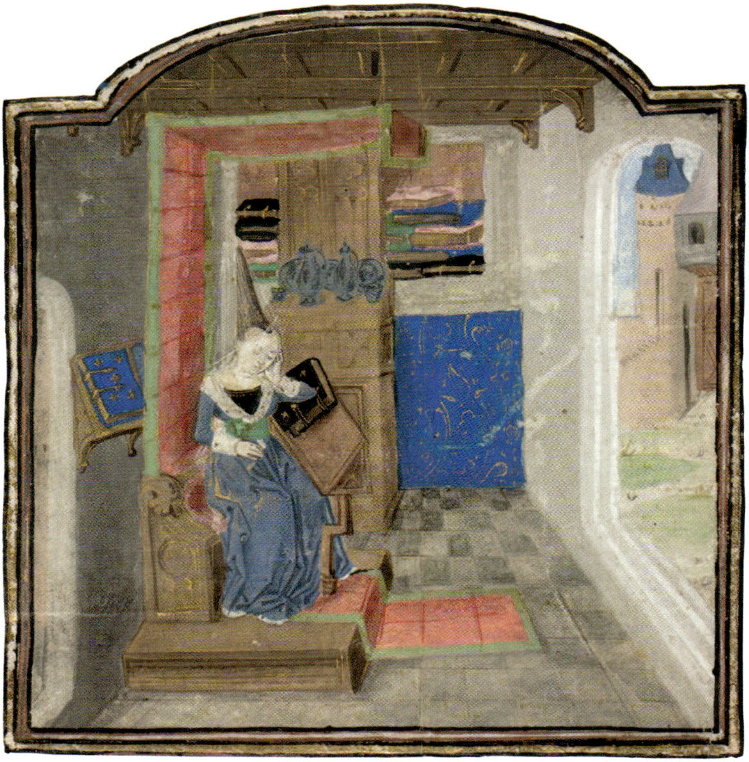

31 Christine de Pisan in her study
Christine de Pisan, *Cité des Dames*. Anonymous Dutch translation
Master of Margaret of York
Bruges, 1475
305 × 210 mm
Add. MS 20698, f. 2

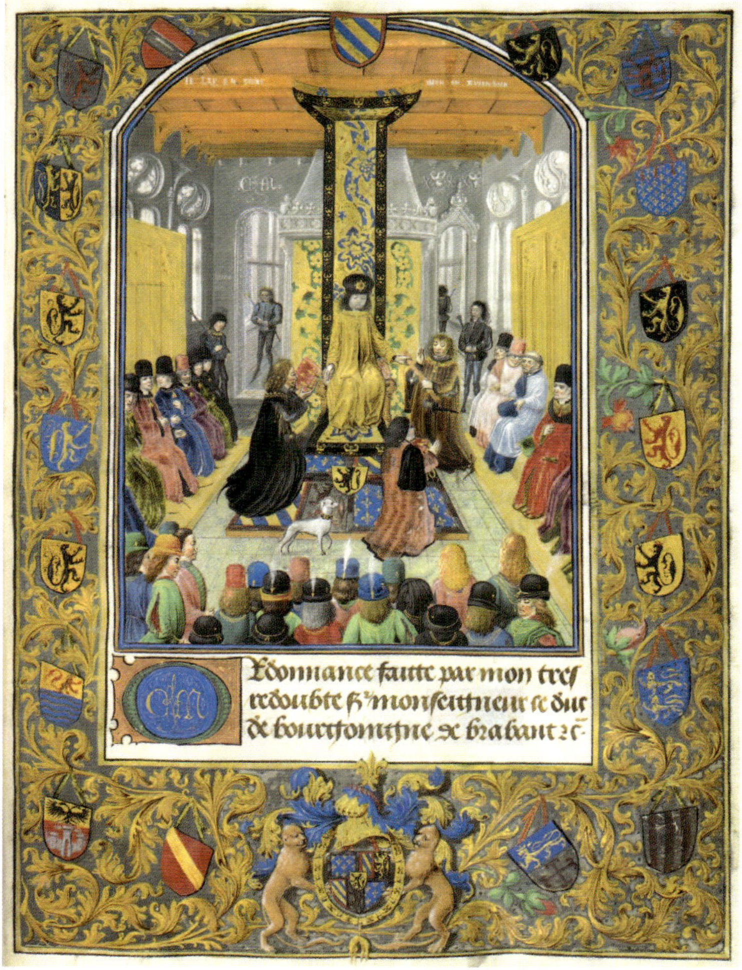

32 Charles the Bold receiving his military captains
Military ordinance of Charles the Bold, Duke of Burgundy
Master of Fitzwilliam 268
Bruges, 1475
305 × 216 mm
Add. MS 36619, f. 5

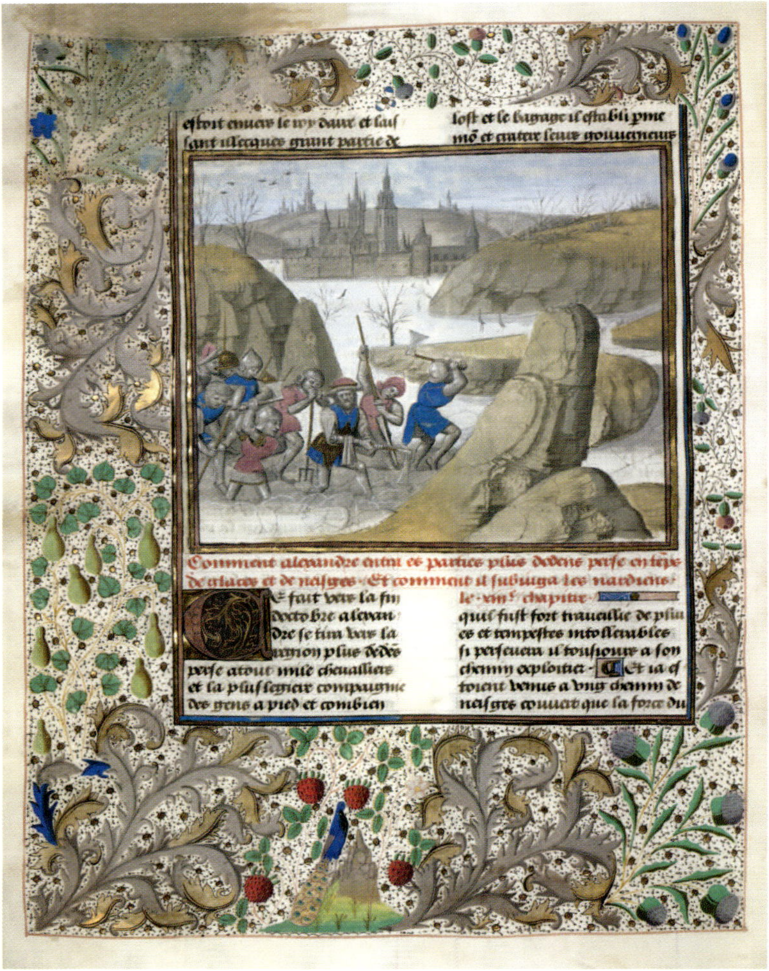

33 Alexander and his army cutting through the ice in Persia
Quintus Curtius Rufus, *Historia Alexandri magni.*
French translation by Vasco da Lucena
Rambures Master, Amiens (?), *c.* 1475–1480
430 × 335 mm
Royal MS 15 D iv, f. 101v

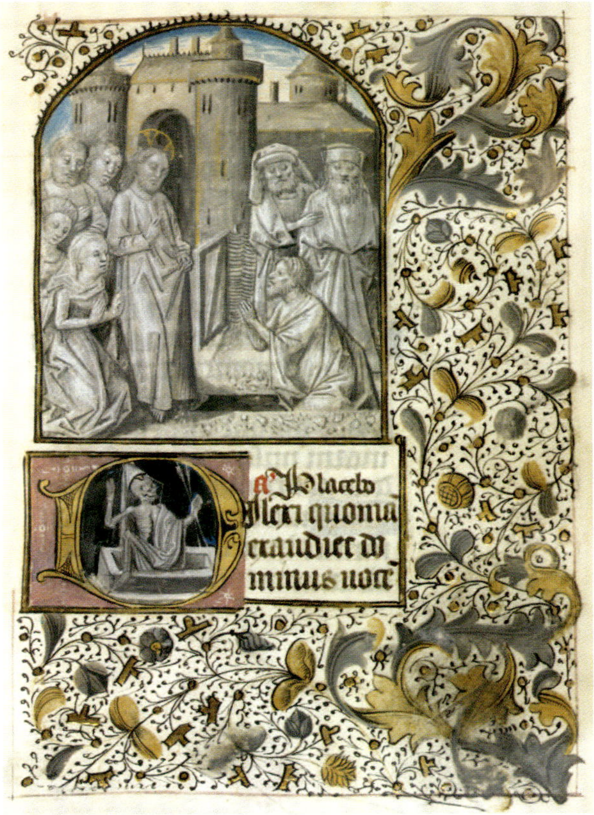

34 Raising of Lazarus
Hours of Marguerite Blondel
Rambures Master
Amiens, c. 1475
175 × 132 mm
Add. MS 19738, f. 128

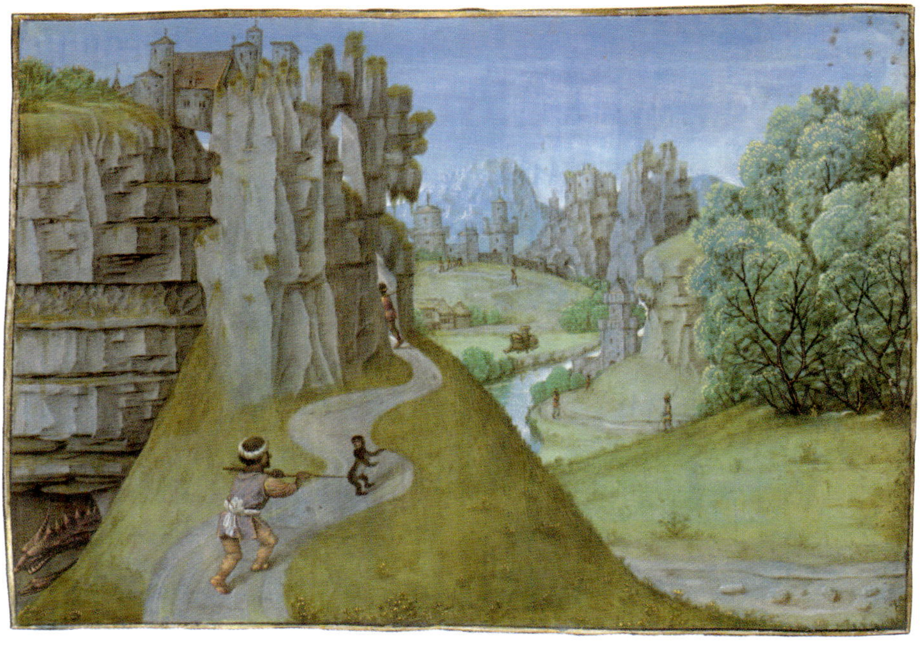

35 *Maritaine in Africa*
Le Trésor des Histoires
Master of the London Wavrin (?)
Bruges, *c.* 1475–1480
480 × 355 mm
Cotton MS Augustus A v, f. 354v (detail)

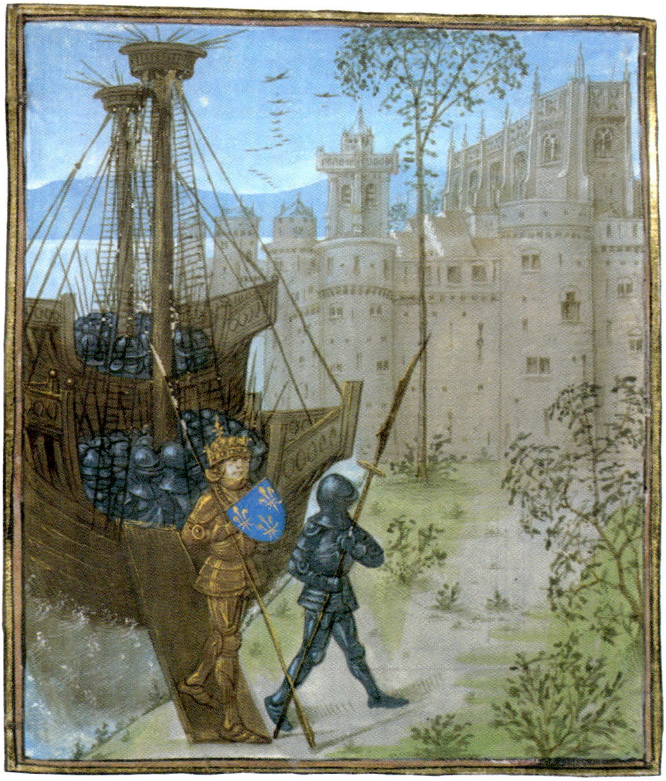

36 French army disembarks in Africa
Jean Froissart, *Chroniques*, vol. 4. Made for Sir Thomas Thwaytes
Master of the London Wavrin (?)
Bruges, *c.* 1475–1480
420 × 315 mm
Royal MS 14 D vi, f. 84v (detail, actual size)

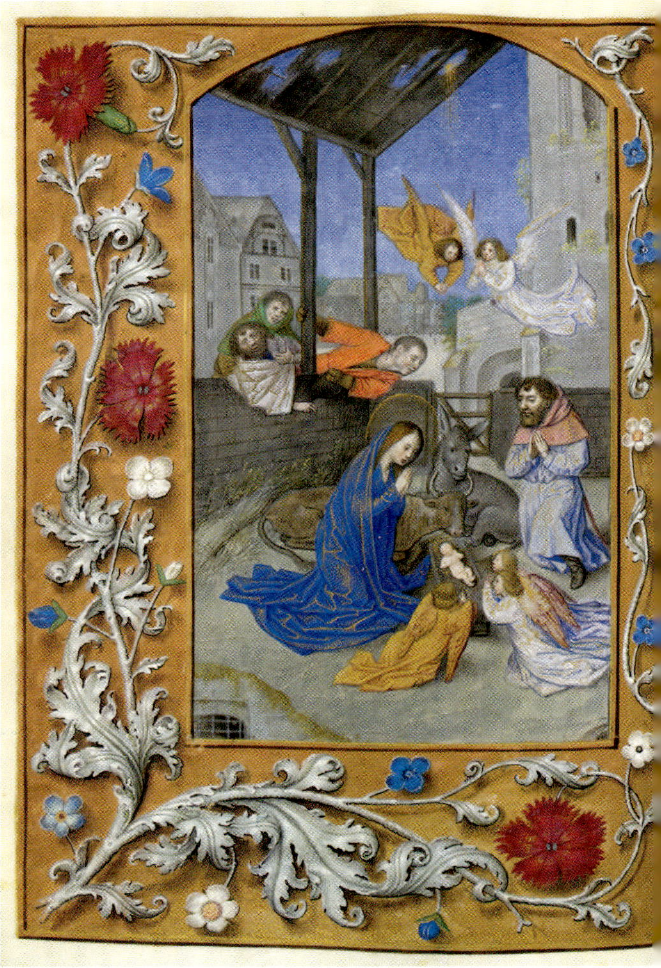

37 & 38 *Nativity* and Prime
London Hours of William Lord Hastings
Master of the First Prayer book of Maximilian
Ghent (?), late 1470s
165 × 125 mm
Add. MS 54782, ff. 106v-107

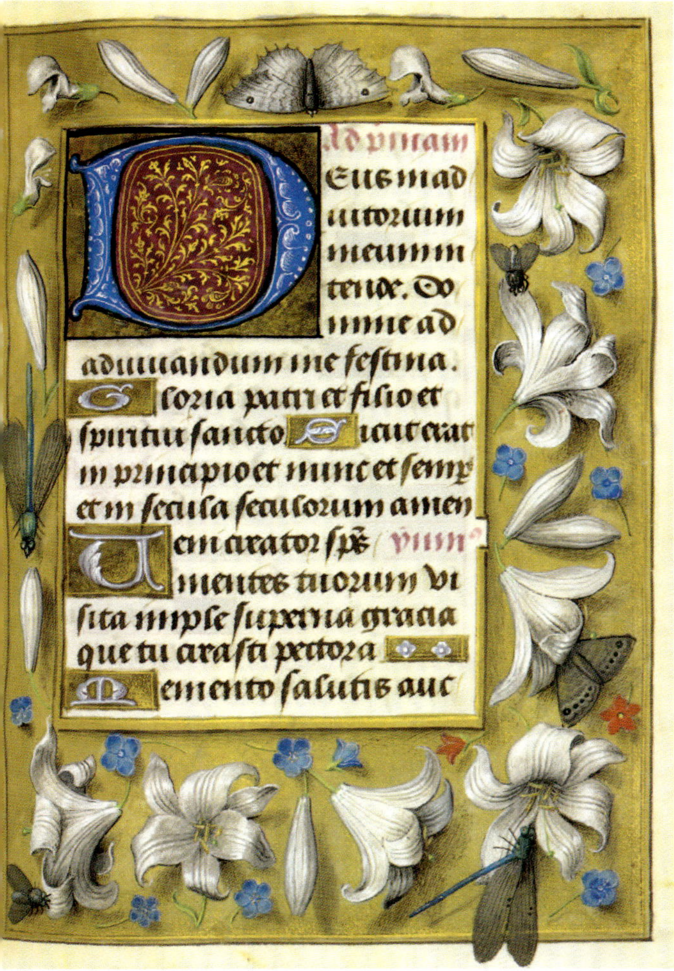
Ad primam
Deus in ad
iutorium
meum in
tende. Do
mine ad
adiuvandum me festina.
Gloria patri et filio et
spiritui sancto. Sicut erat
in principio et nunc et semp
et in secula seculorum amen
Veni creator sps ymn
mentes tuorum vi
sita imple superna gracia
que tu creasti pectora
Memento salutis auc

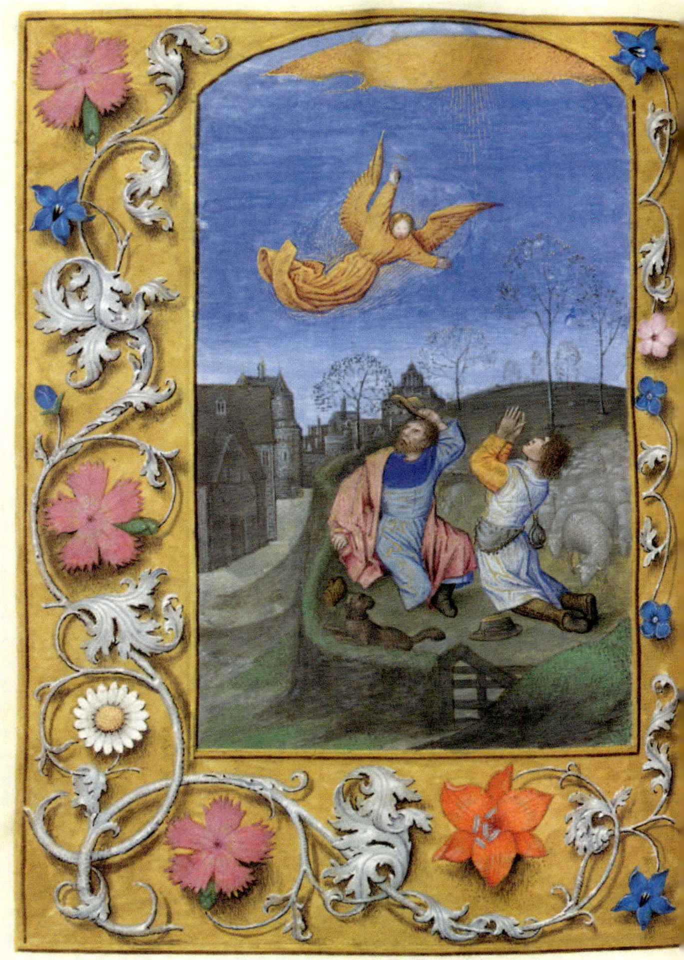

39 & 40 Annunciation to the Shepherds and Terce
London Hours of William Lord Hastings
Master of the First Prayer book of Maximilian
Ghent (?), late 1470s
165 × 125 mm
Add. MS 54782, ff. 113v-114

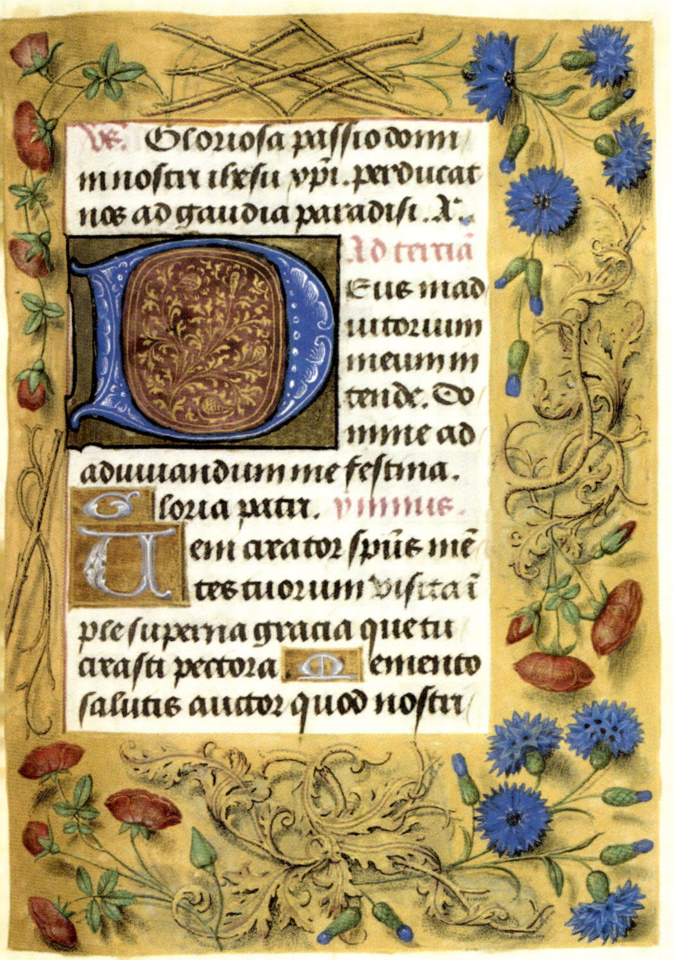
℟. Gloriosa passio domi
ni nostri ihesu xpi. perducat
nos ad gaudia paradisi. ℣.
Ad terciā
Deus in ad
iutorium
meum in
tende. Do
mine ad
adiuvandum me festina.
Gloria patri. hymnus.
Veni creator spūs mē
tes tuorum visita ī
ple superna gracia que tu
creasti pectora. Memento
salutis auctor quod nostri

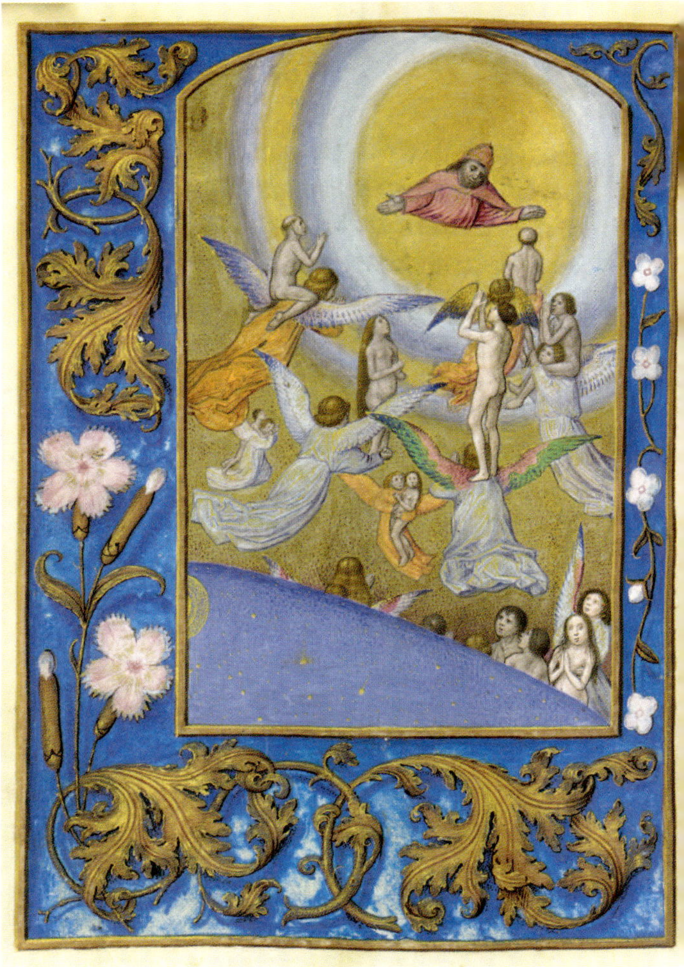

41 & 42 *Souls of the blessed arriving in Heaven* and Commendation of Souls
London Hours of William Lord Hastings
Master of the First Prayer book of Maximilian
Ghent (?), late 1470s
165 × 125 mm
Add. MS 54782, ff. 230-231

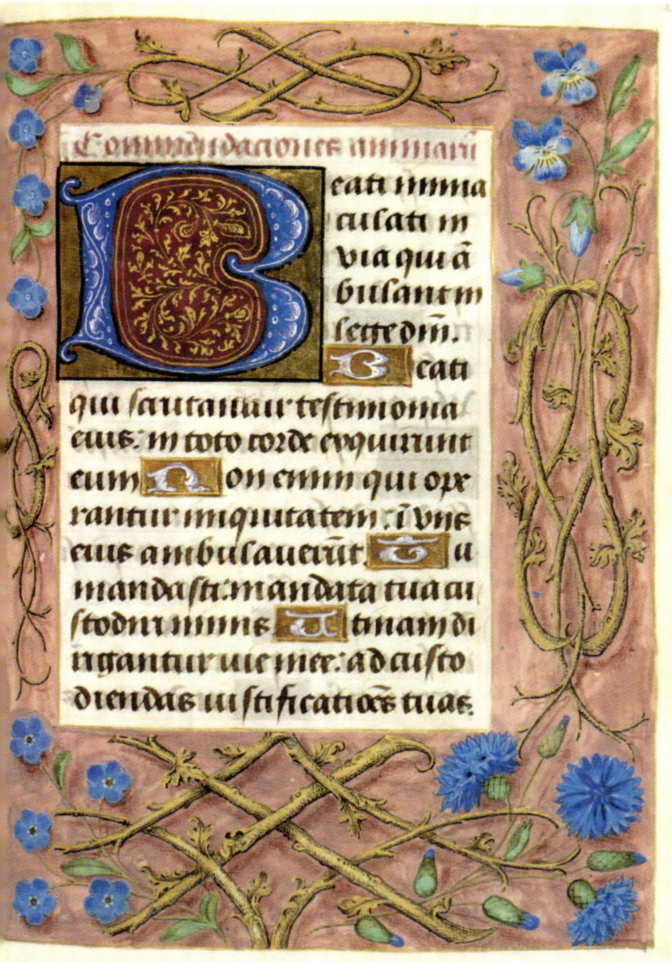

Commendaciones animarum

Beati imma
culati in
via qui am
bulant in
lege dni. Beati
qui scrutantur testimonia
eius: in toto corde exquirunt
eum. Non enim qui ope
rantur iniquitatem: in vias
eius ambulaverunt. Tu
mandasti: mandata tua cu
stodiri nimis. Utinam di
rigantur vie mee: ad custo
diendas iustificationes tuas.

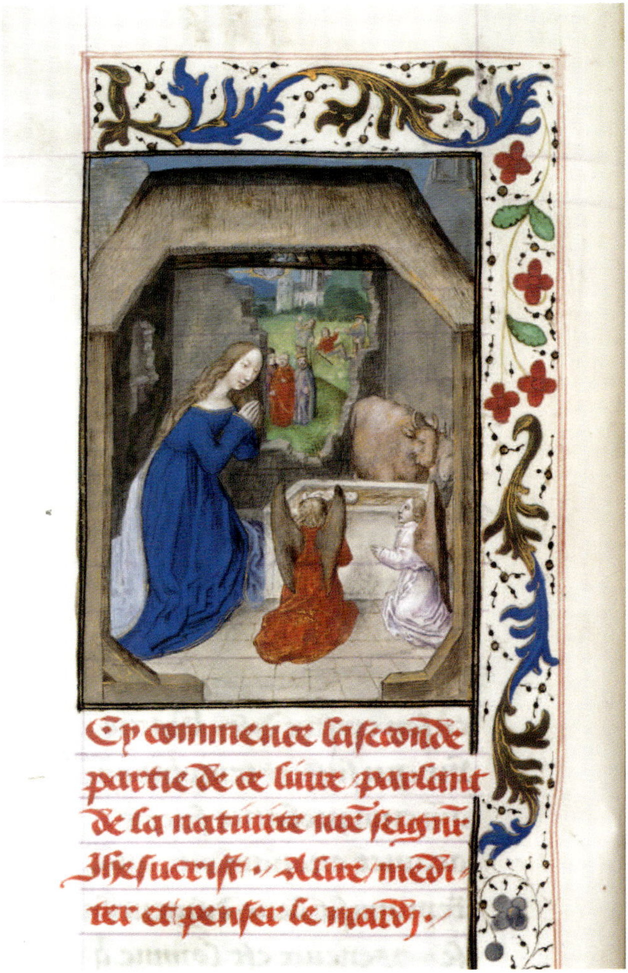

43 Nativity
Vie de Jésus-Christ
Master of the Flemish Boethius
Ghent, 1479
390 × 280 mm
Royal MS 16 G.iii, f. 33v (detail)

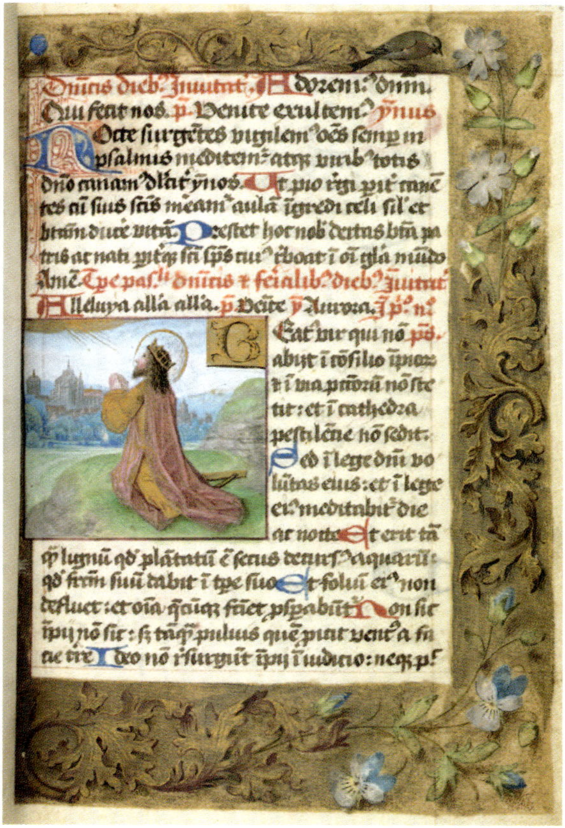

44 *David in prayer*
Breviary for the use of the 'Rooclooster', near Brussels
Circle of the Vienna Master of Mary of Burgundy
Brussels and Ghent, *c.* 1477
127 × 89 mm
Add. MS 18863, f. 23 (actual size)

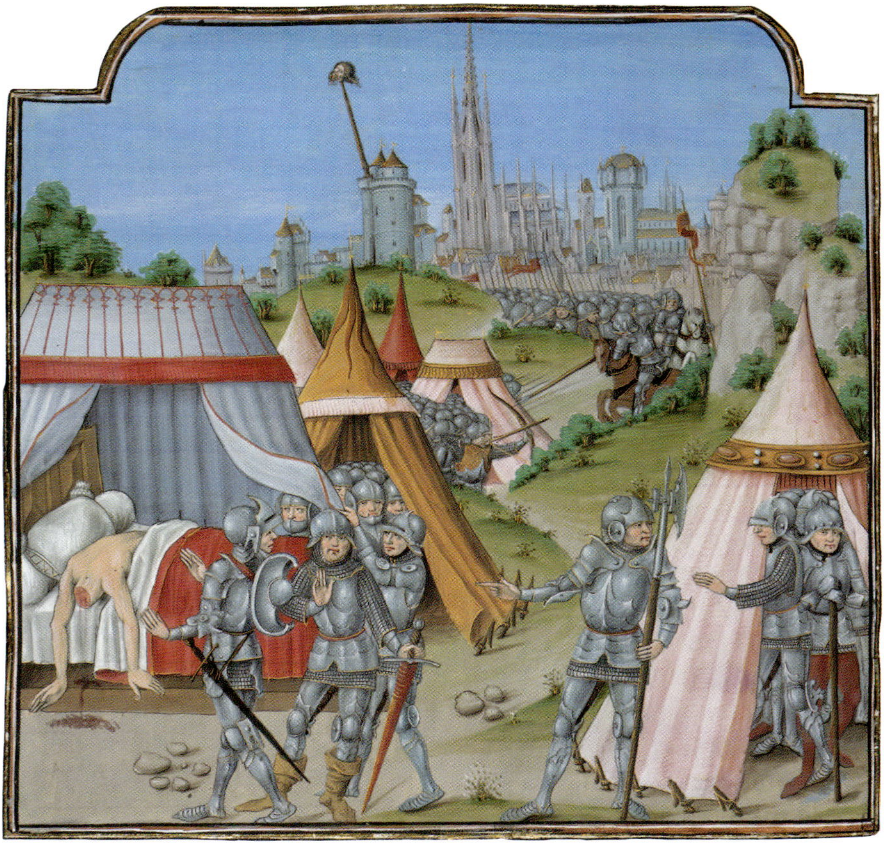

45 *Discovery of the body of Holofernes*
Bible Historiale of Edward IV
Master of the Soane Josephus
Bruges, *c.* 1479
435 × 320 mm
Royal MS 15 D i, f. 76v (detail)

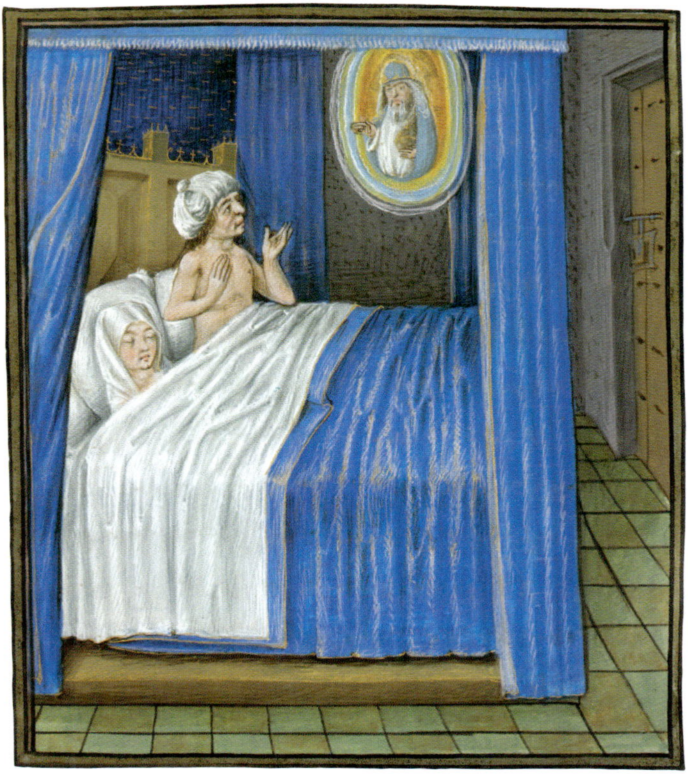

46 *Amram's Dream*
Vincent of Beauvais, *Speculum Historiale*. French translation by Jean de Vignay.
Made for Edward IV of England
Master of Edward IV, Bruges, *c.* 1478–1480
470 × 345 mm
Royal MS 14 E i, vol. 1, f. 77 (detail)

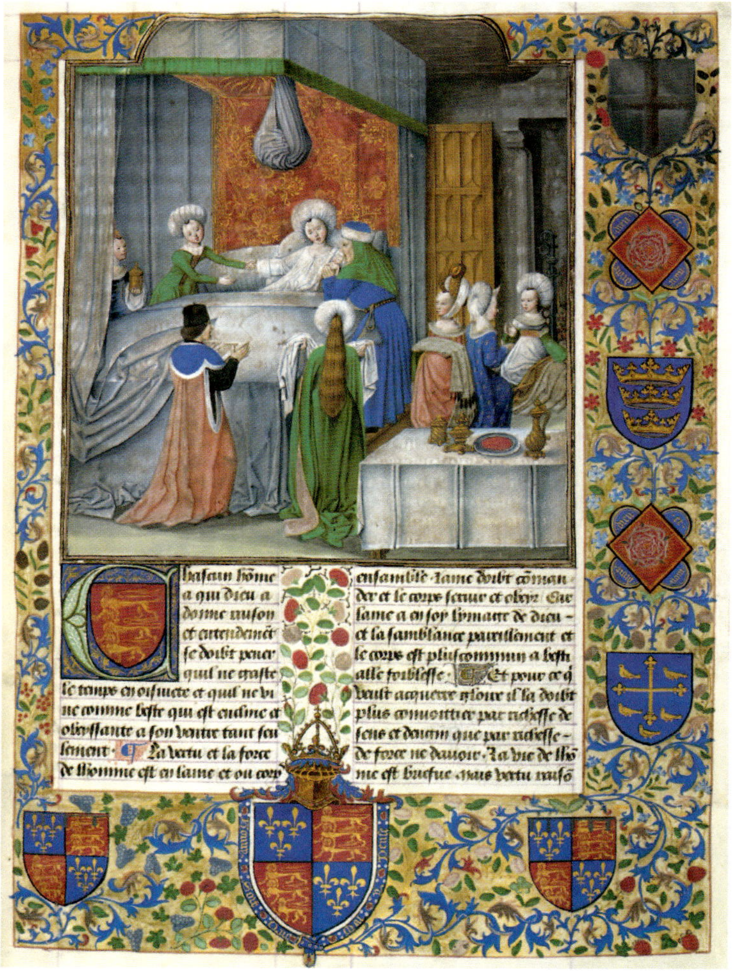

47 *Birth of Julius Caesar*
Grande Histoire Cesar made for Edward IV of England
Bruges, 1479
480 × 335 mm
Royal MS 17 F ii, f. 9

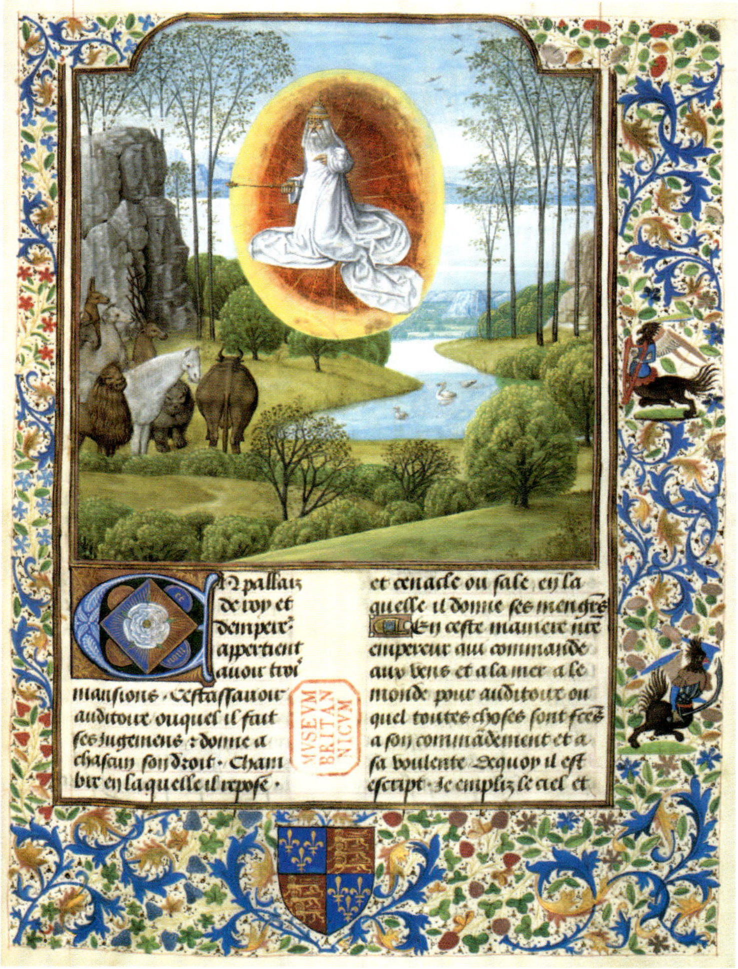

48 *Creation*
Bible Historiale of Edward IV
Bruges, 1479
430 × 313 mm
Royal MS 18 D ix, f. 5

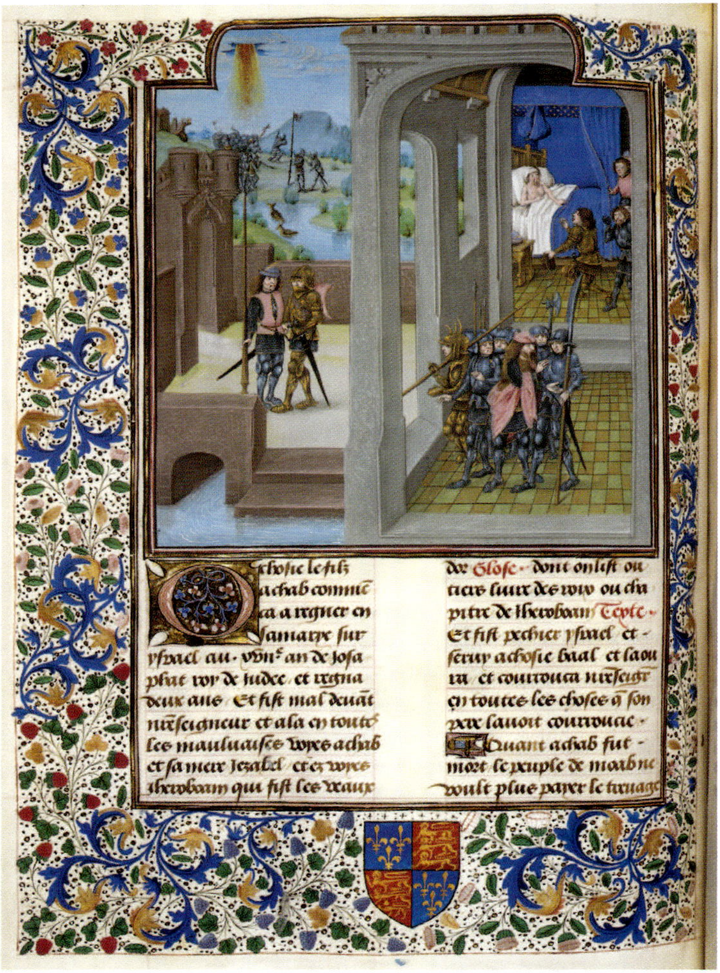

49 *Elijah bringing down fire on the soldiers of Ahaziah*
Bible Historiale of Edward IV
Master of Edward IV
Bruges, 1479
430 × 313 mm
Royal MS 18 D x, f. 115v

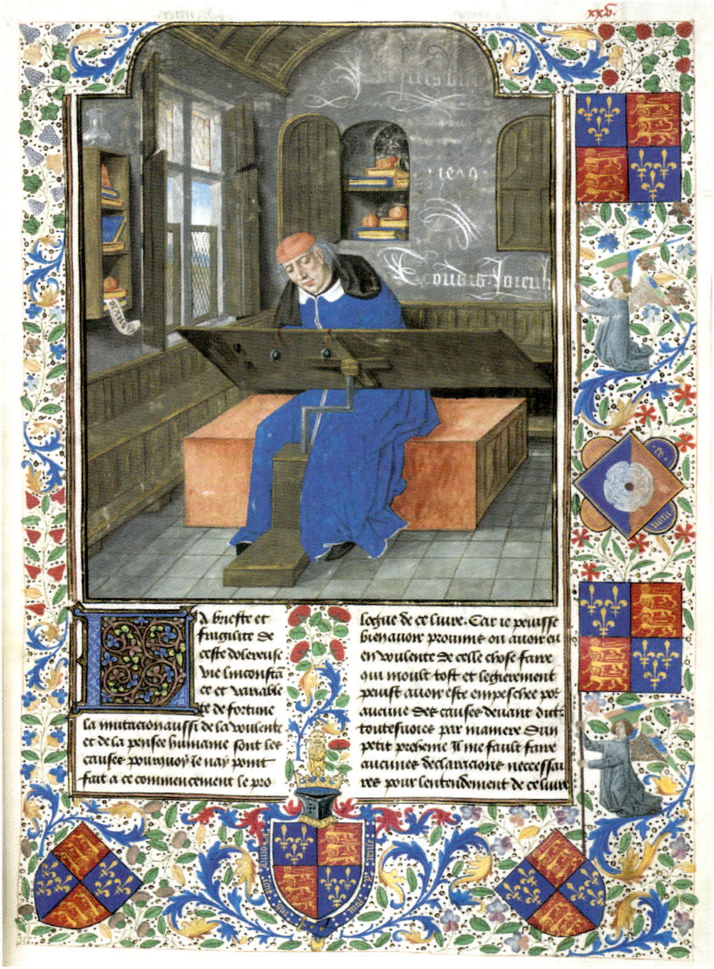

50 *The translator in his study*
Valerius Maximus, *Facta et Dicta Memorabilia*. Volume 1. French translation by Simon de Hesdin and Nicolas de Gonesse. Made for Edward IV of England
Master of the White Inscriptions, Bruges, 1479
480 × 340 mm
Royal MS 18 E iii, f. 2

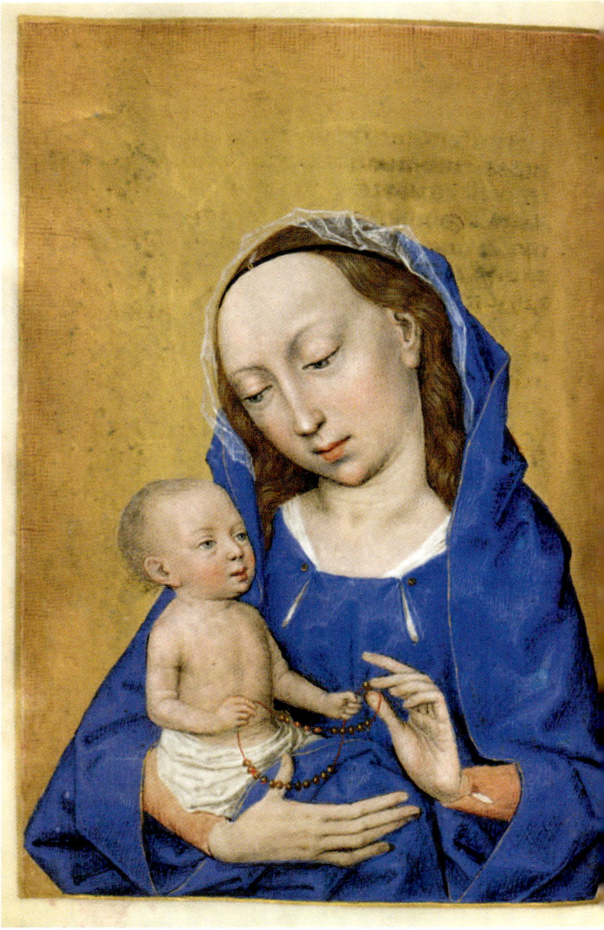

51 & 52 *Virgin and Child* and Advent Mass of the Virgin
Huth Hours
Simon Marmion
Valenciennes, *c.* 1480
148 × 116 mm
Add. MS 38126, ff. 102v-103

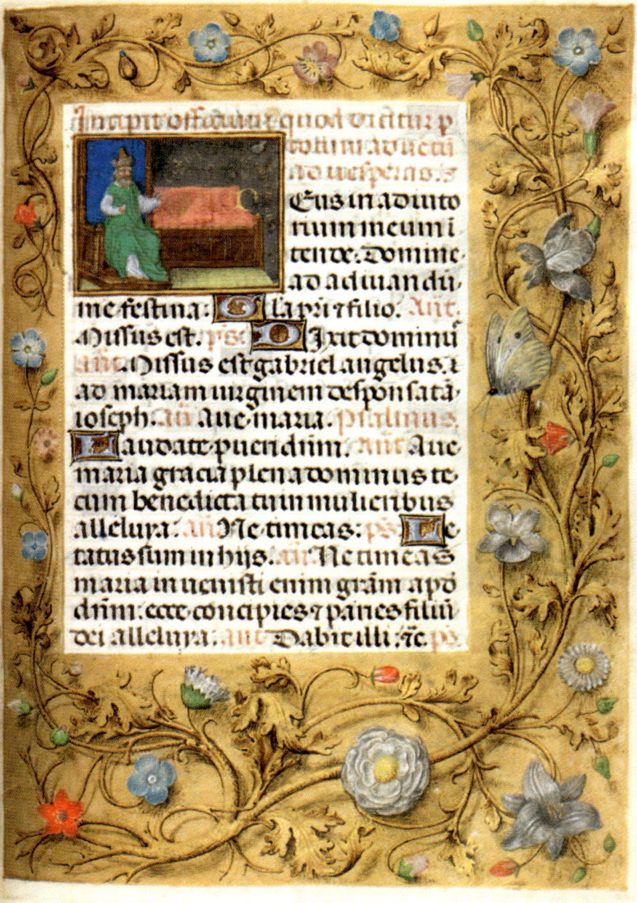
Incipit officium quod dicitur p
totum in adventu
ad vesperas.
Deus in adiuto
rium meum i
tende. Domine
ad adiuvandu
me festina. Gloria patri et filio. Ant.
Missus est. Ps. Dixit dominu
Ant. Missus est gabriel angelus a
ad mariam virginem desponsata
ioseph. Ant. Ave maria. Psalmus.
Laudate pueri dnm. Ant. Ave
maria gratia plena dominus te
cum benedicta tu in mulieribus
alleluya. Ant. Ne timeas. Ps. Le
tatus sum in hijs. Ant. Ne timeas
maria invenisti enim gram apd
dnm: ecce concipies et paries filiu
dei alleluya. Ant. Dabit illi &c. Ps.

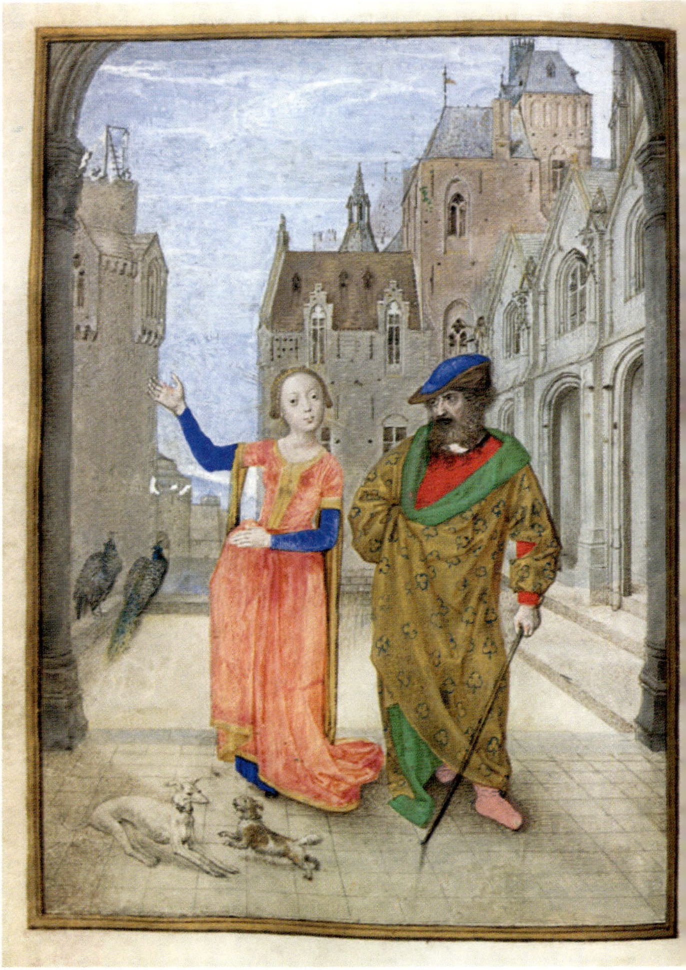

53 & 54 *Disputation of St Barbara* and *Execution of St Barbara*
Huth Hours
Master of the Houghton miniatures and assistant of Simon Marmion
Ghent and Valenciennes, *c.* 1480
148 × 116 mm
Add. MS 38126, ff. 145v-146

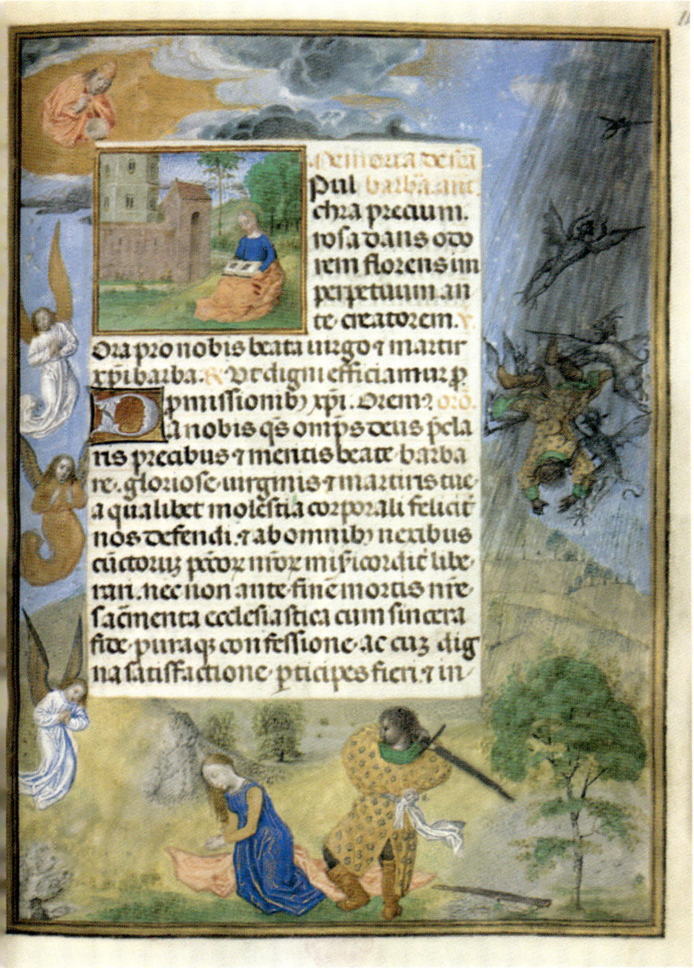
Memoria de sancta
pul barbara ant.
chra precaum.
rosa dans odo
rem florens in
perpetuum an
te creatorem. V.
Ora pro nobis beata virgo et martir
xpi barbara. R. Ut digni efficiamur p
promissionibus xpi. Oremus. Oro.
Da nobis quesumus omnipotens deus pela
ns precibus et meritis beate barba
re gloriose virginis et martiris tue
a qualibet molestia corporali feliciter
nos defendi et ab omnibus necibus
cunctorum peccatorum misericordie libe
rari necnon ante finem mortis nostre
sacramenta ecclesiastica cum sincera
fide puraque confessione ac cum dig
na satisfactione percipere fieri et in

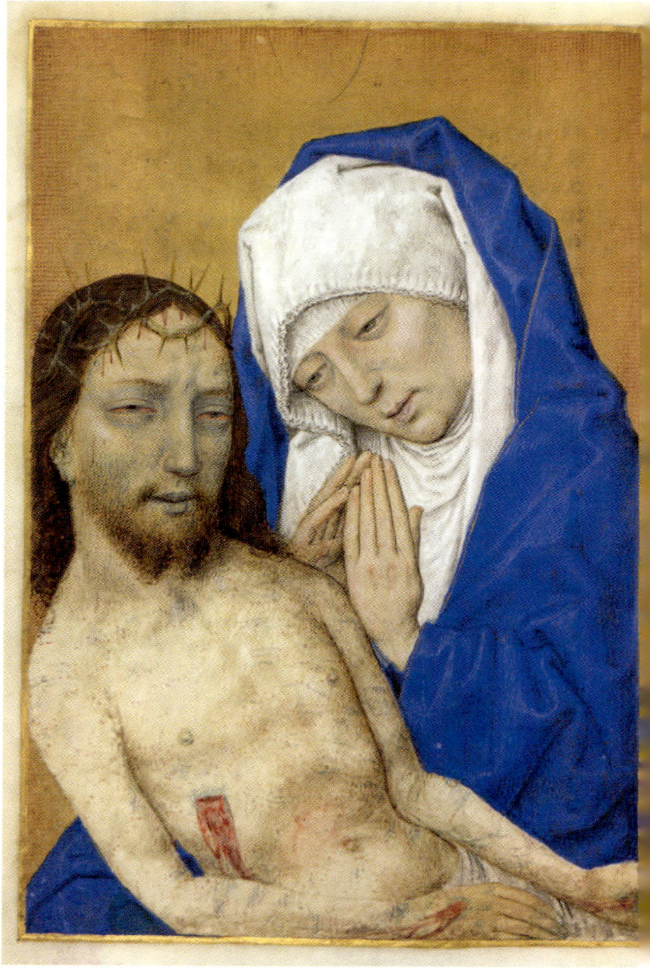

55 & 56 *Virgin and dead Christ* and Prayer 'Obsecro te'
Huth Hours
Simon Marmion
Valenciennes, *c.* 1480
148 × 116 mm
Add. MS 38126, ff. 240v-241

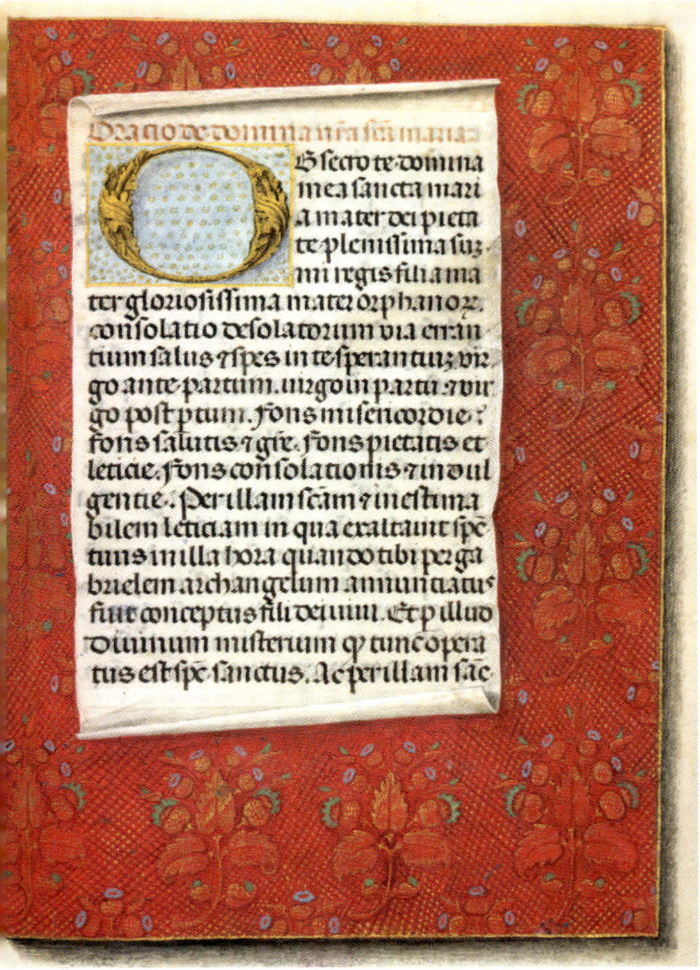
Oratio de domina nrã scã maria

Obsecro te domina
mea sancta mari
a mater dei pieta
te plenissima sũ
mi regis filia ma
ter gloriosissima mater orphanoꝝ
consolatio desolatorum via erran
tium salus et spes in te sperantiuz vir
go ante partum. uirgo in partu et vir
go post ptum. fons misericordie et
fons salutis et grẽ. fons pietatis et
leticie. fons consolationis et indul
gentie. Per illam scãm et inestima
bilem leticiam in qua exultauit spũ
tuus in illa hora quando tibi per ga
brielem archangelum annunciatus
fuit conceptus filii dei uiui. Et p illud
diuinum misterium qd tunc opera
tus est spũs sanctus. Ac per illam sãc

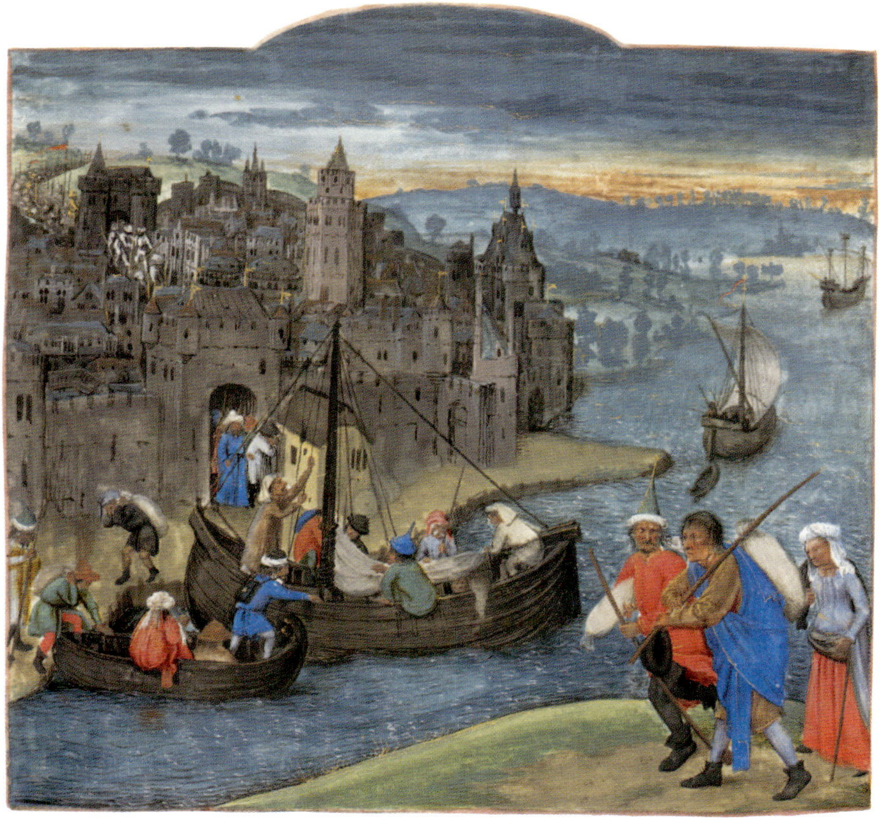

57 *The Gauls escaping their city by night*
Julius Caesar, *Commentarii*. French translation by Jan du Quesne
Bruges, *c.* 1480
365 × 260 mm
Egerton MS 1065, f. 116v (detail)

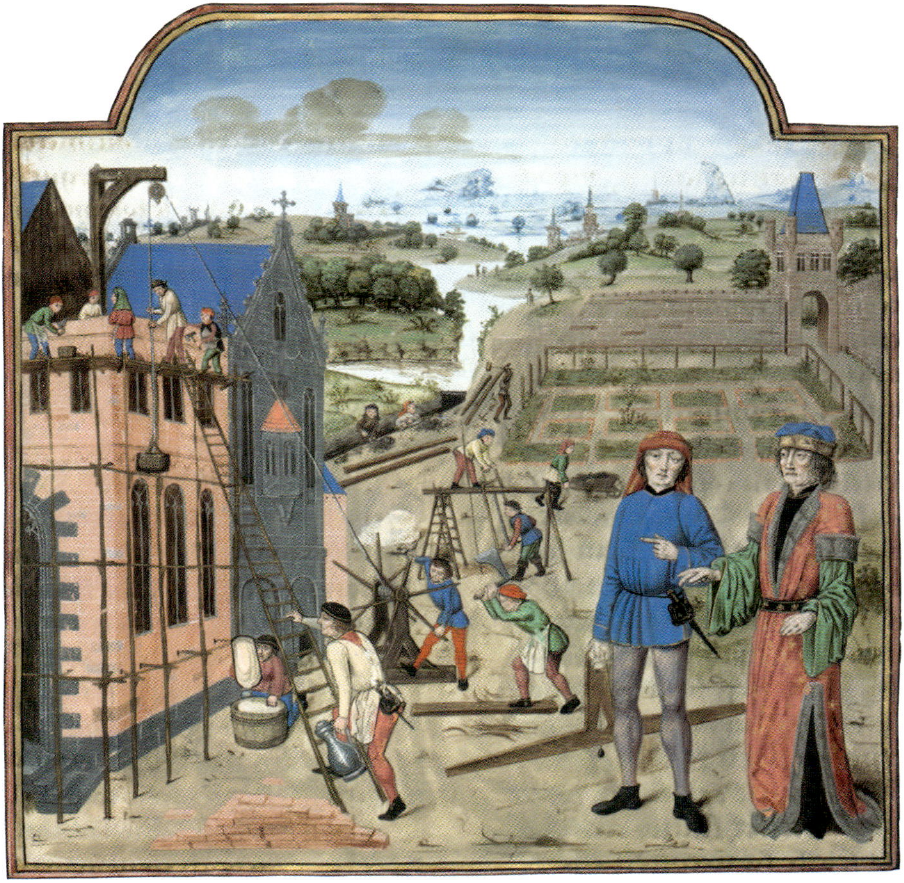

58 *Tasks in the town and country*
Petrus de Crescentiis, *Ruralium commodorum libri XII.*
Anonymous French translation
Master of 1482, Bruges, c. 1480
480 × 360 mm
Add. MS 19720, f. 27 (detail)

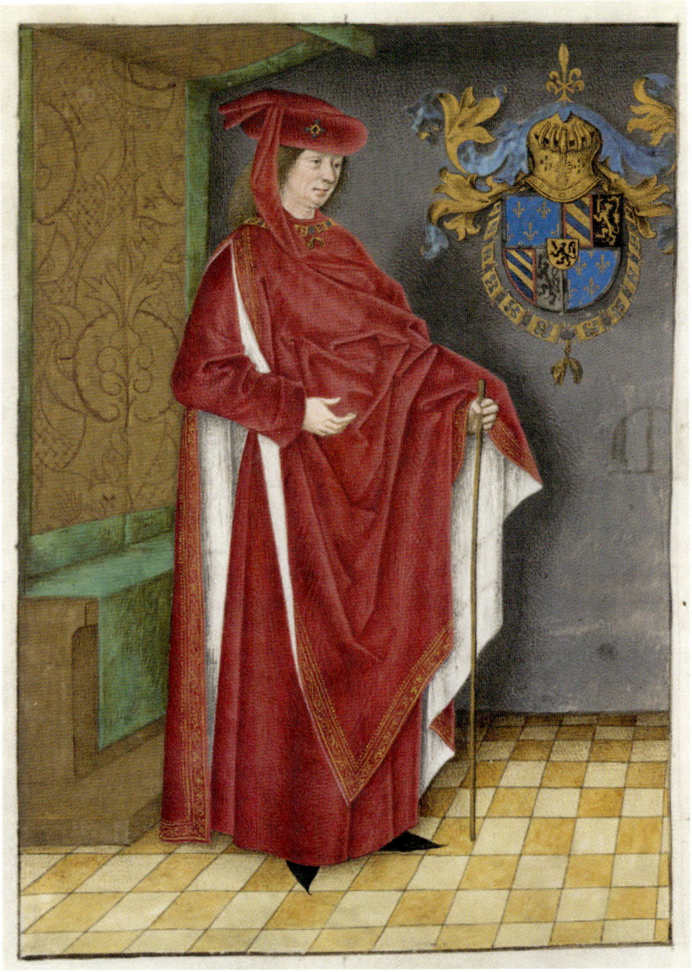

59 *Philip the Good as patron of the Order*
Statutes and Armorial of the Order of the Golden Fleece.
Made for Jean de Lannoy, Abbot of St Bertin
Circle of the Master of the London Wavrin, Bruges, between 1481 and 1486
255 × 190 mm
Harley MS 6199, f. 57v

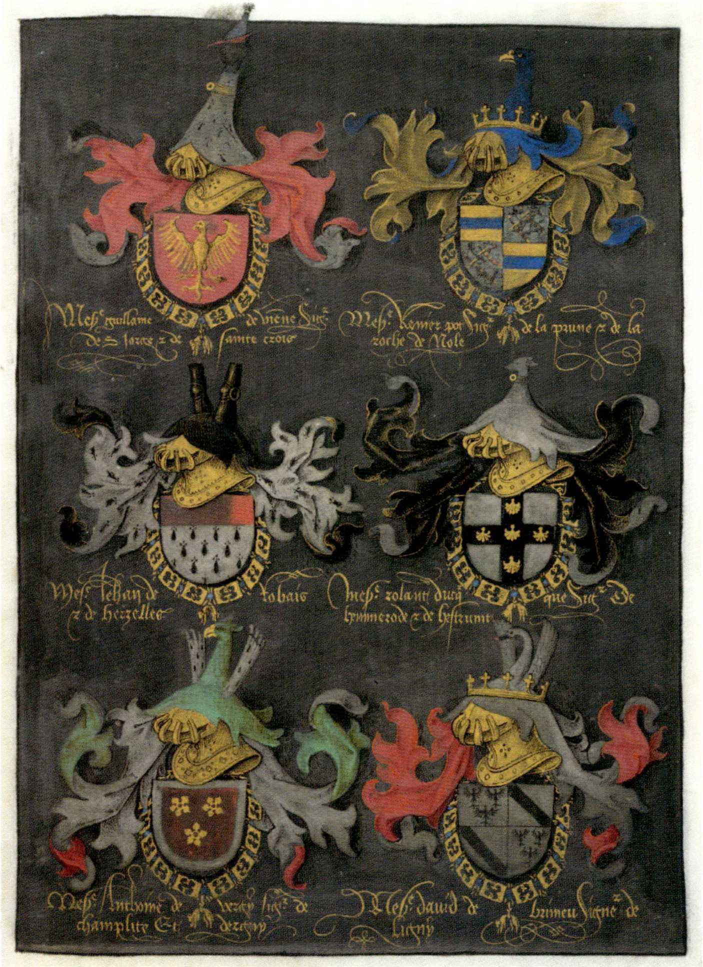

60 *Achievements of arms of the first knights of the Order of the Golden Fleece*
Statutes and Armorial of the Order of the Golden Fleece.
Made for Jean de Lannoy, Abbot of St Bertin
Circle of the Master of the London Wavrin, Bruges, between 1481 and 1486
255 × 190 mm
Harley MS 6199, f. 59

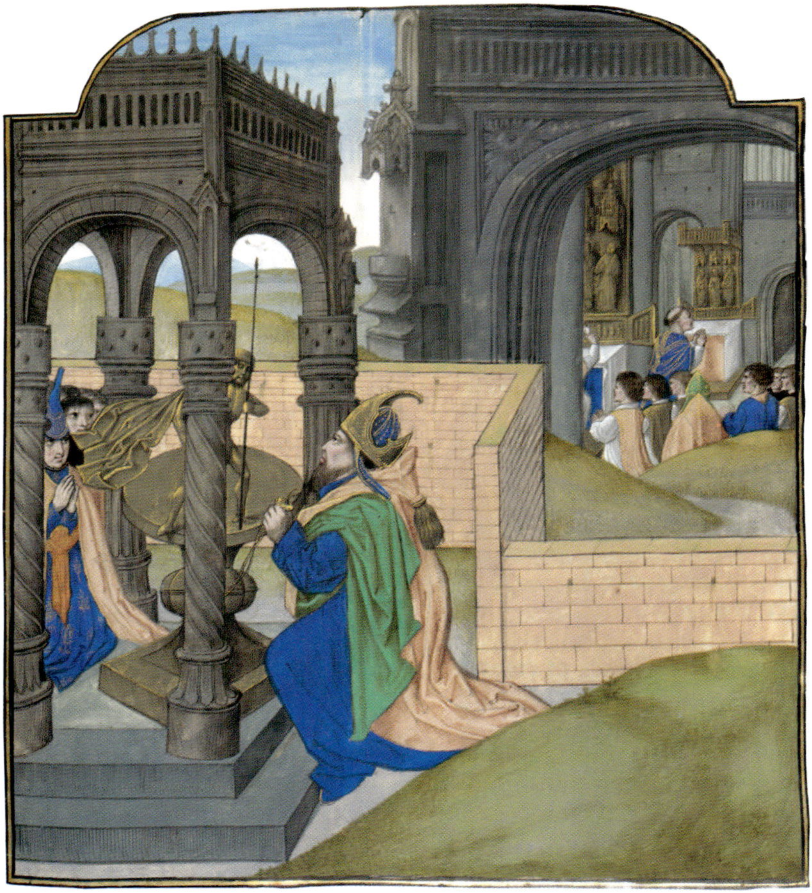

61 *Pagan and Christian worship*
St Augustine, *De Civitate Dei*.
French translation by Raoul des Presles. Made for Edward IV of England
Master of the White Inscriptions
Bruges, *c.* 1480, 475 × 335 mm
Royal MS 17 F iii, vol. 2, f. 120 (detail)

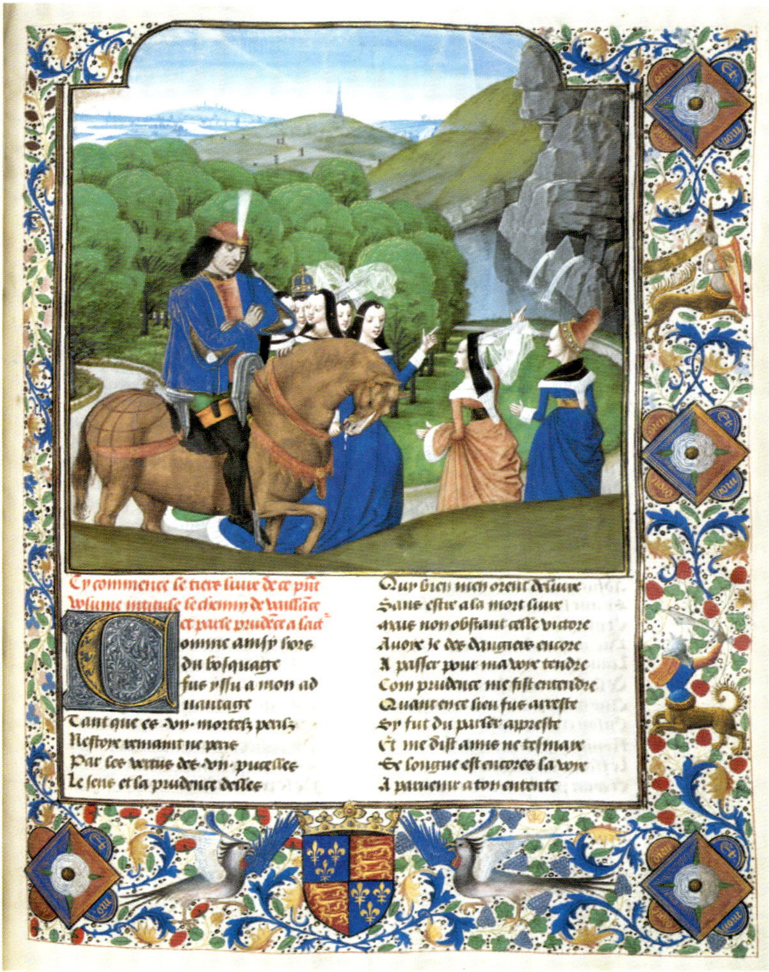

62 *The Seven Virtues leading the author from the forest of Temptation*
Jean de Courcy, *Chemin de vaillance*. Made for Edward IV of England
Master of the White Inscriptions
Bruges, *c.* 1480
468 × 345 mm
Royal MS 14 E ii, f. 194

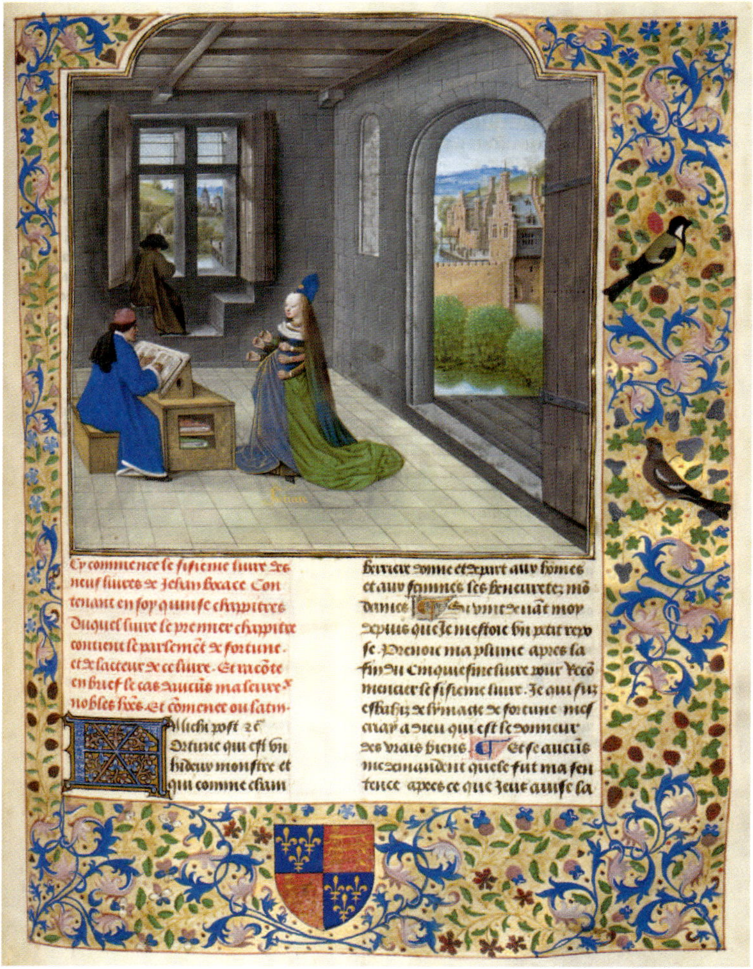

63 *Fortune appearing to Boccaccio*
Giovanni Boccaccio, *De casibus illustrium virorum et feminarum.*
French translation by Laurent du Premierfait. Made for Edward IV of England.
Master of the Getty Froissart, Bruges, *c.* 1480
480 × 340 mm
Royal MS 14 E v, f. 291

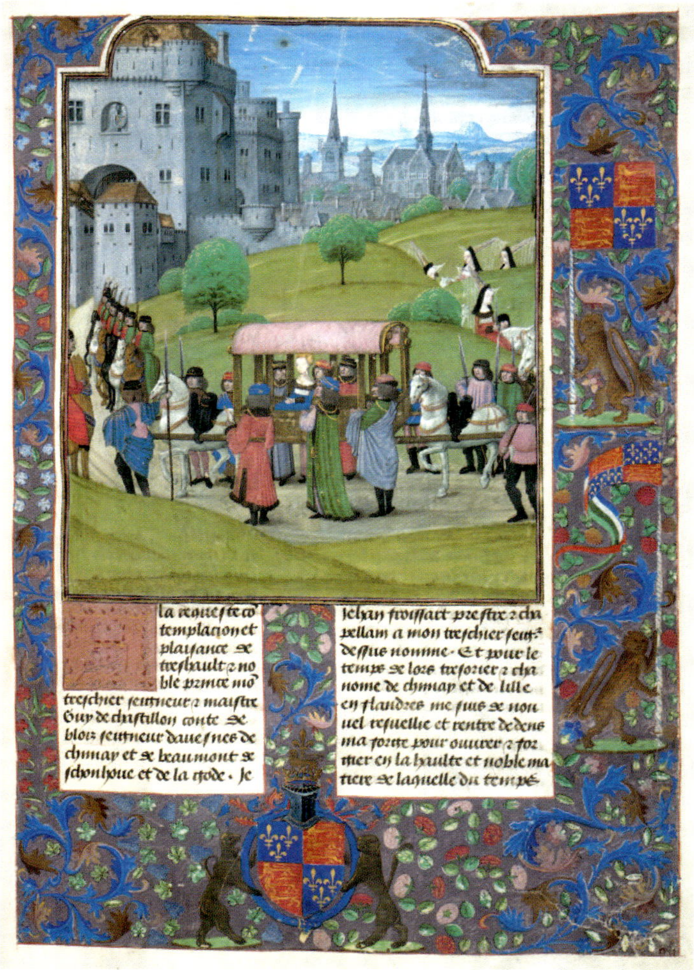

64 *Entry of Isabel of Bavaria into Paris*
Jean Froissart, *Chroniques*. Made for Edward IV of England
Master of the Getty Froissart
Bruges, c. 1480
475 × 355 mm
Royal MS 18 E.ii, f. 7

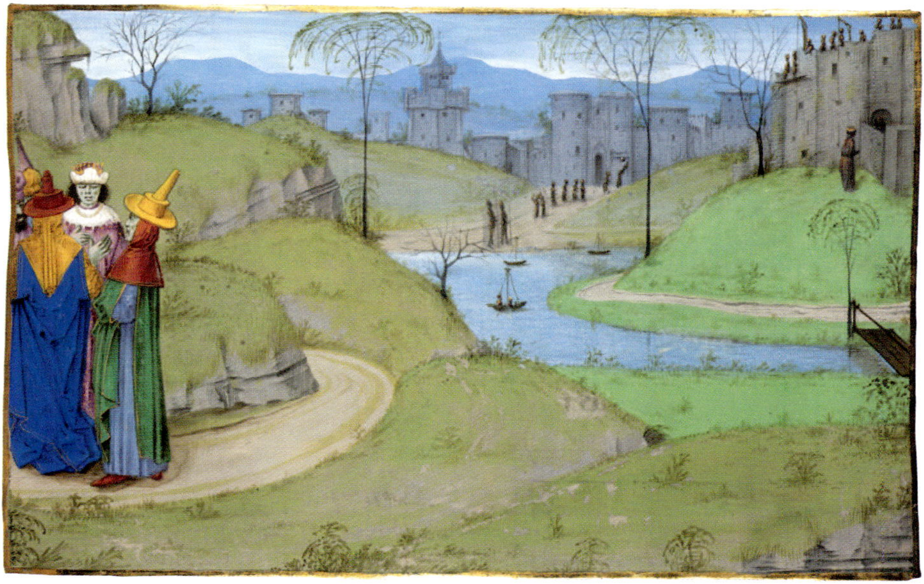

65 *Vortigern consulting the magicians*
Jean de Wavrin, *Recueil des croniques et anciennes istoires de la Grant Bretaigne*, Vol. I.
Made for Edward IV of England
Master of the London Wavrin, Bruges, *c.* 1480
450 × 350 mm
Royal MS 15 E iv, vol. I, f. 93 (detail)

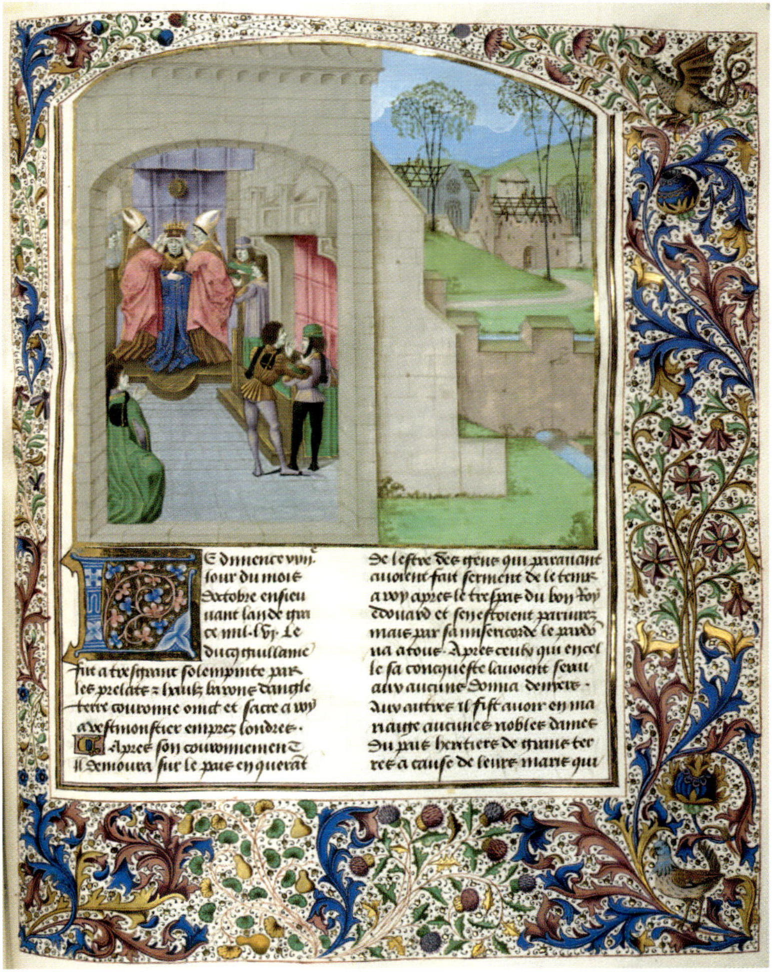

66 *Coronation of William the Conqueror*

Jean de Wavrin, *Recueil des croniques et anciennes istoires de la Grant Bretaigne*, Vol. I.

Made for Edward IV of England

Master of the London Wavrin, Bruges, *c.* 1480

450 × 350 mm

Royal MS 15 E.iv, vol. 2, f. 236

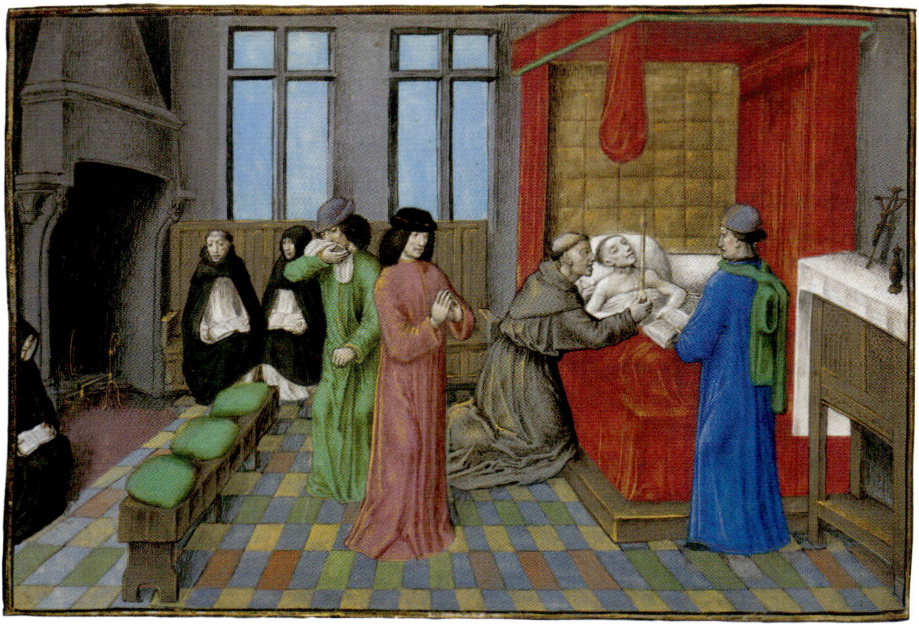

67 *Death of Godfrey of Bouillon*
William of Tyre, *Historia rerum in partibus transmarinis gestarum.*
French translation and continuation to 1232
Master of the Flemish Boethius, Bruges, *c.* 1480
470 × 342 mm
Royal MS 15 E i, f. 150v (detail)

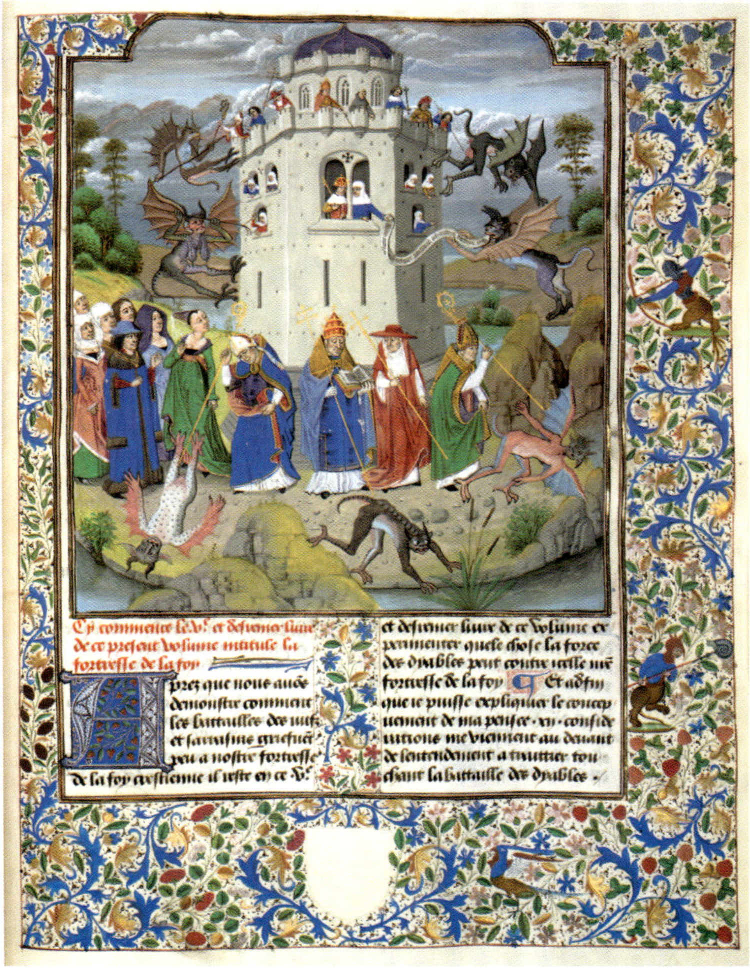

68 The Fortress of Faith defended against devils
Alfonso de Spina, *Fortalitum fidei*. French translation by Pierre Richard
Follower of Loyset Liédet
Bruges, c. 1480
510 × 375 mm
Royal MS 17 F vii, f. 129

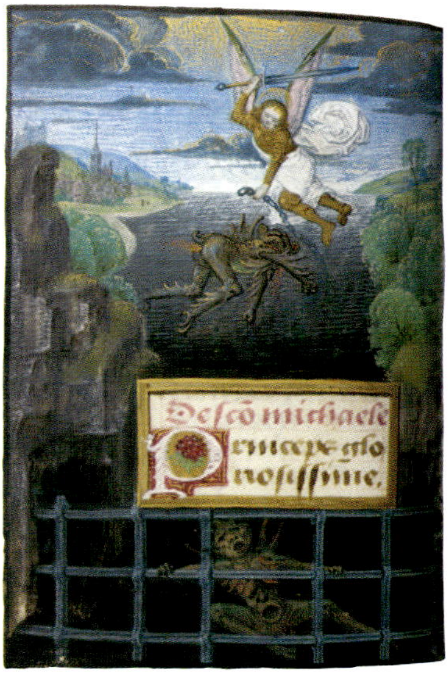

69 *St Michael defeating Lucifer*
Book of Hours, use of Rome
Master of the Dresden Prayer Book
Bruges, *c.* 1480–1485
88 × 62 mm
Egerton MS 2045, f. 254v (actual size)

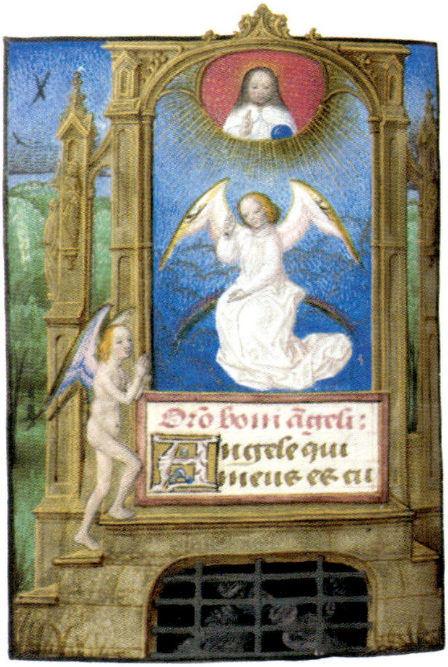

70 *Soul approaching its good angel*
Book of Hours, use of Rome
Master of the Dresden Prayer Book
Bruges, c. 1480–1485
88 × 62 mm
Egerton MS 2045, f. 260v (actual size)

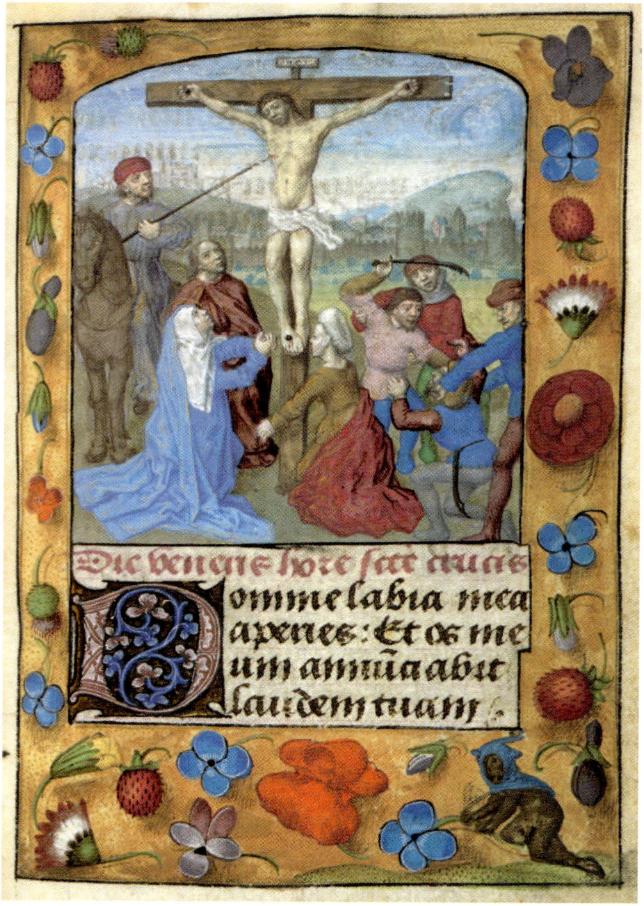

71 *Crucifixion*
Book of Hours, use of Rome
Circle of the Vienna Master of Mary of Burgundy
Ghent (?), 1480s
135 × 93 mm
Add. MS 17026, f. 43 (actual size)

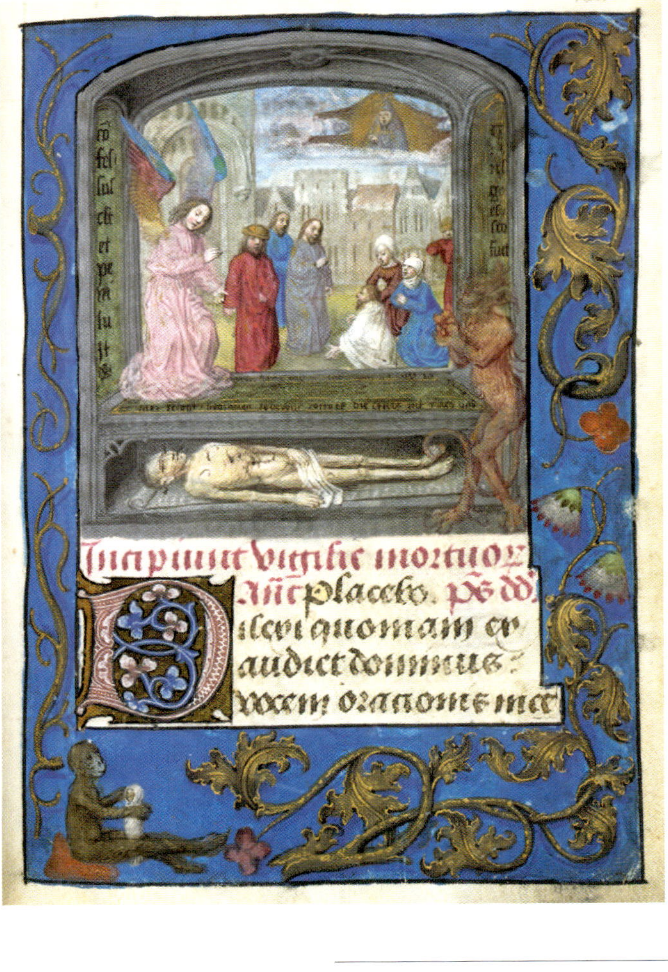

72 *Raising of Lazarus*
Book of Hours, use of Rome
Circle of the Vienna Master of Mary of Burgundy
Ghent (?), 1480s
135 × 93 mm
Add. MS 17026, f. 152 (actual size)

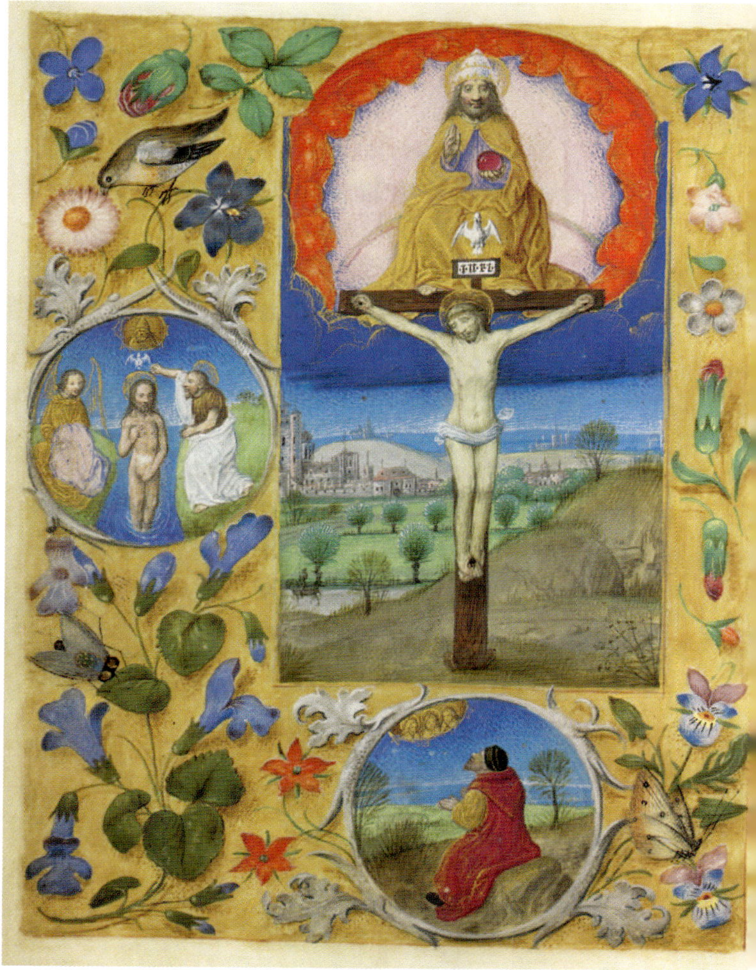

73 *Trinity, Baptism of Christ and Prophet adoring the Trinity*
So-called Hours of Philip the Fair
Master of the Dresden Prayer book
Bruges, 1480s
150 × 110 mm
Add. MS 17280, f. 24v

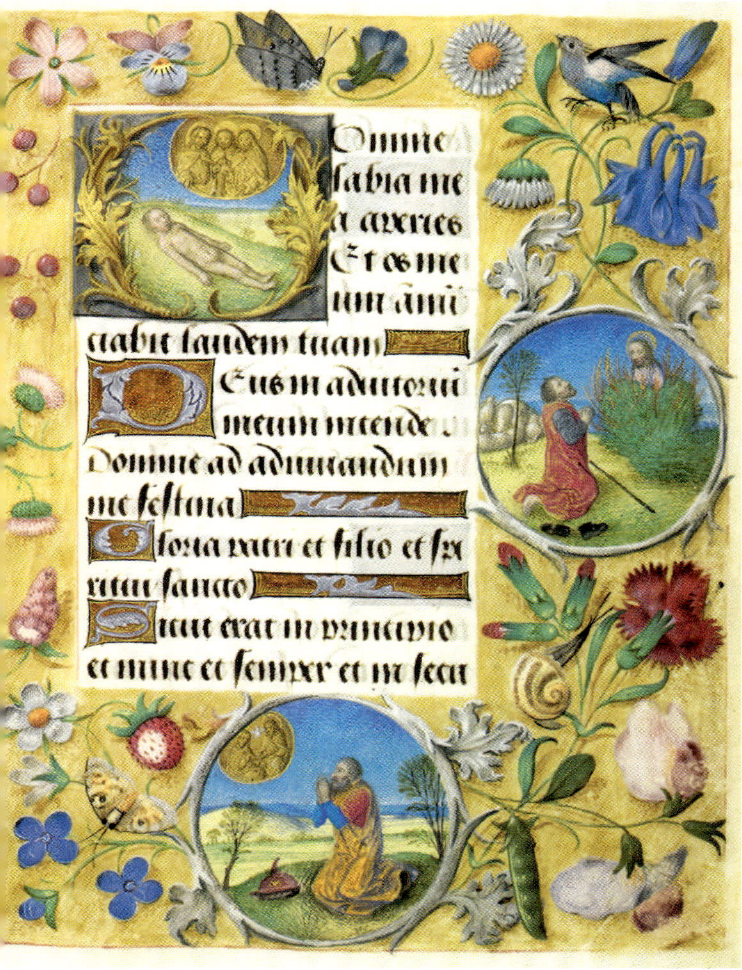

74 *Trinity regarding Adam*, *Moses and the burning bush* and *Prophet adoring the Trinity* and Monday Hours
So-called Hours of Philip the Fair
Master of the Dresden Prayer book, Bruges, 1480s
150 × 110 mm
Add. MS 17280, f. 25

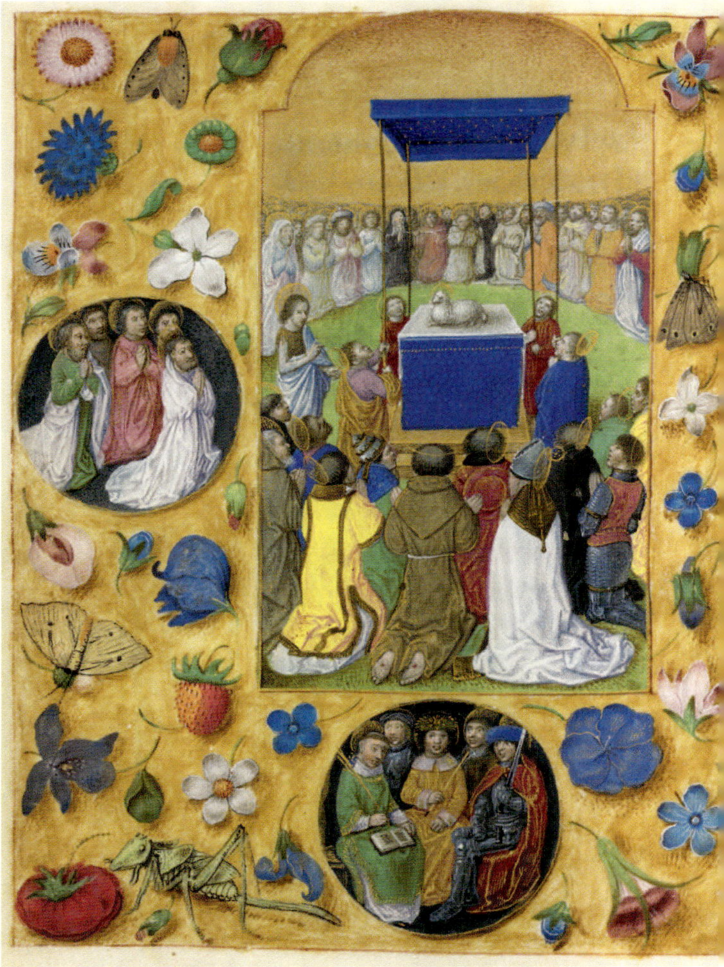

75 & 76 *Adoration of the Lamb* and Wednesday Hours
So-called Hours of Philip the Fair
Master of the Dresden Prayer book
Bruges, 1480s
150 × 110 mm
Add. MS 17280, ff. 77v-78

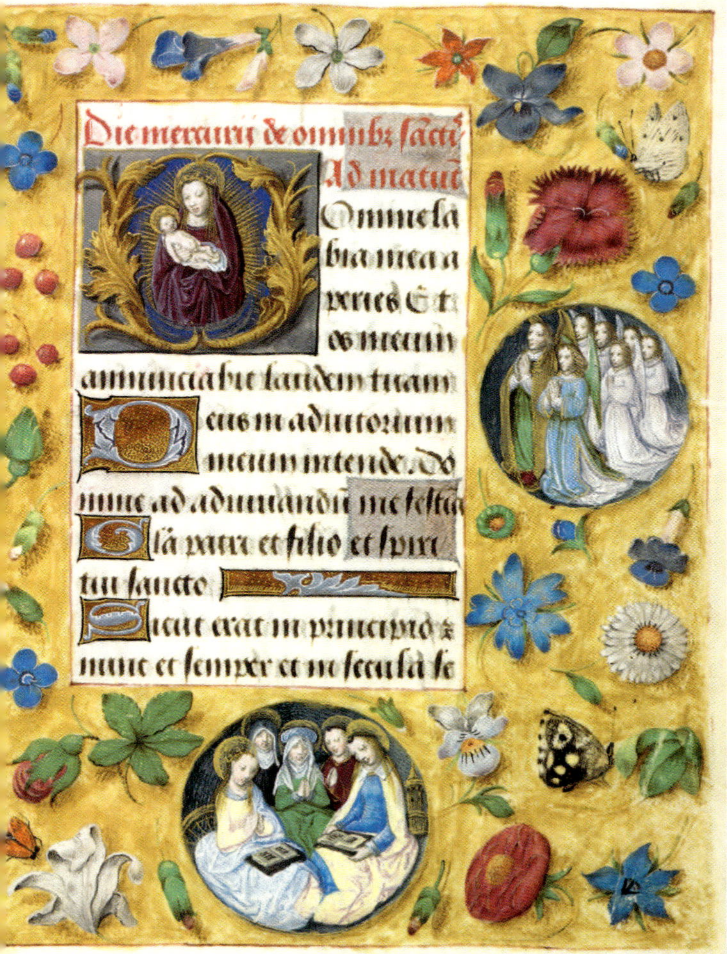
Die mercurij de omnibz sancti[s]
Ad matutĩ
omine la
bia mea a
peries Et
os meum
annunciabit laudem tuam
eus in adiutorium
meum intende. Do
mine ad adiuuandũ me festina
lã patri et filio et spiri
tui sancto
icut erat in principio &
nunc et semper et in seculã se

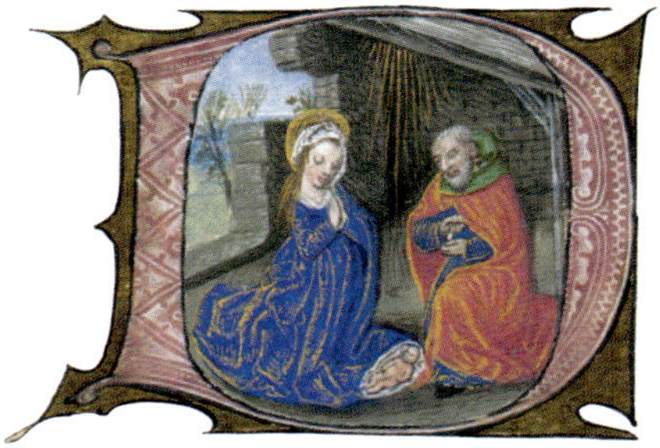

77 *Nativity*
Psalter of Pierre Vaillant (d. 1492)
Master of the Dresden Prayer book
Bruges, 1482
200 × 135 mm
Add. MS 16969, f. 19v (detail, actual size)

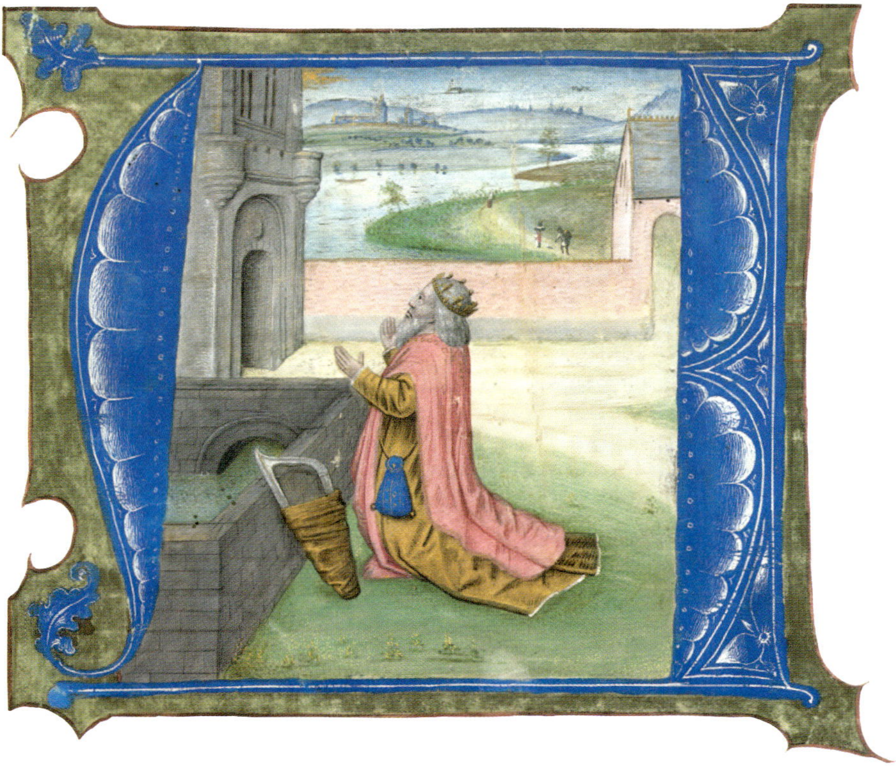

78 David in prayer
Leaf from a Gradual presented by Margaret of York,
dowager Duchess of Burgundy, to the Grey Friars, Greenwich
Follower of the Master of Mary of Burgundy, Ghent, c. 1482
442 × 299 mm
Arundel MS 71, f. 9 (detail)

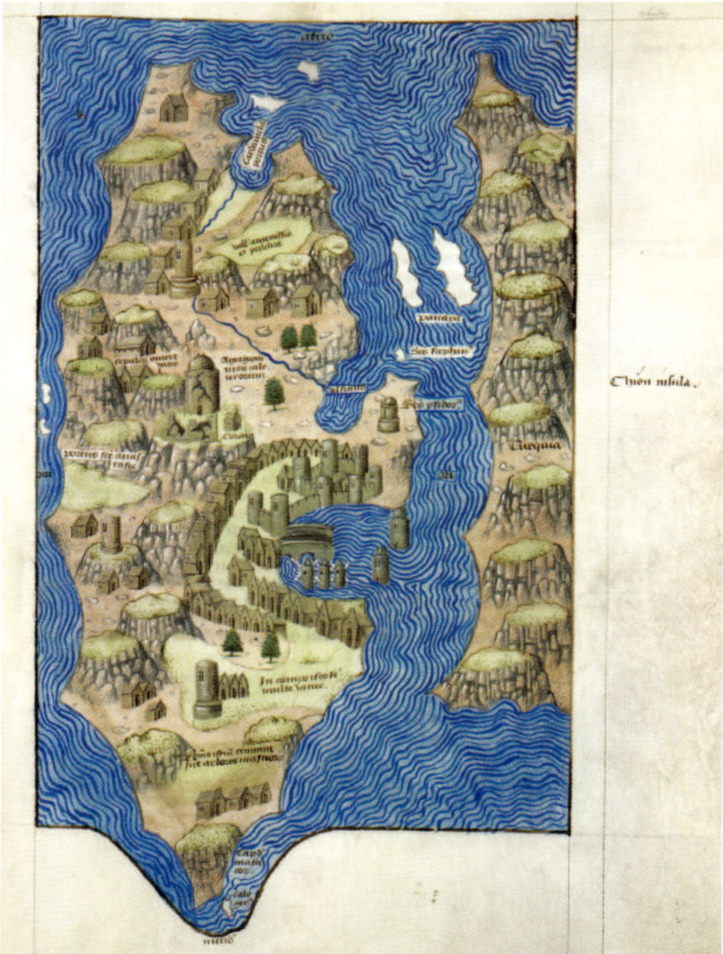

79 The Island of Chios
Christoforo Buondelmonte, *Liber insularum Cycladum*.
Made for Raphael de Mercatellis, Abbot of St Bavon, Ghent
Ghent, *c.* 1482–1485
360 × 255 mm
Arundel MS 93, f. 150

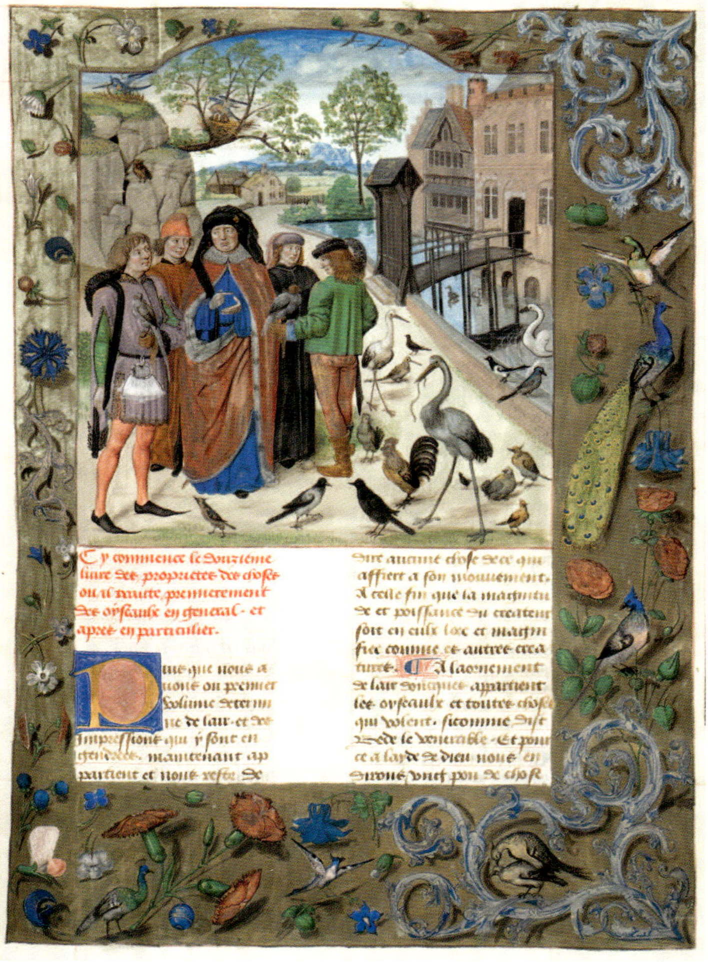

80 *Bartholomaeus Anglicus and the birds*
Bartholomaeus Anglicus, *De proprietatibus rerum.*
French translation by Jean Corbechon
Master of 1482, Bruges, 1482 or shortly afterwards
470 × 345 mm
Royal MS 15 E iii, f. 11

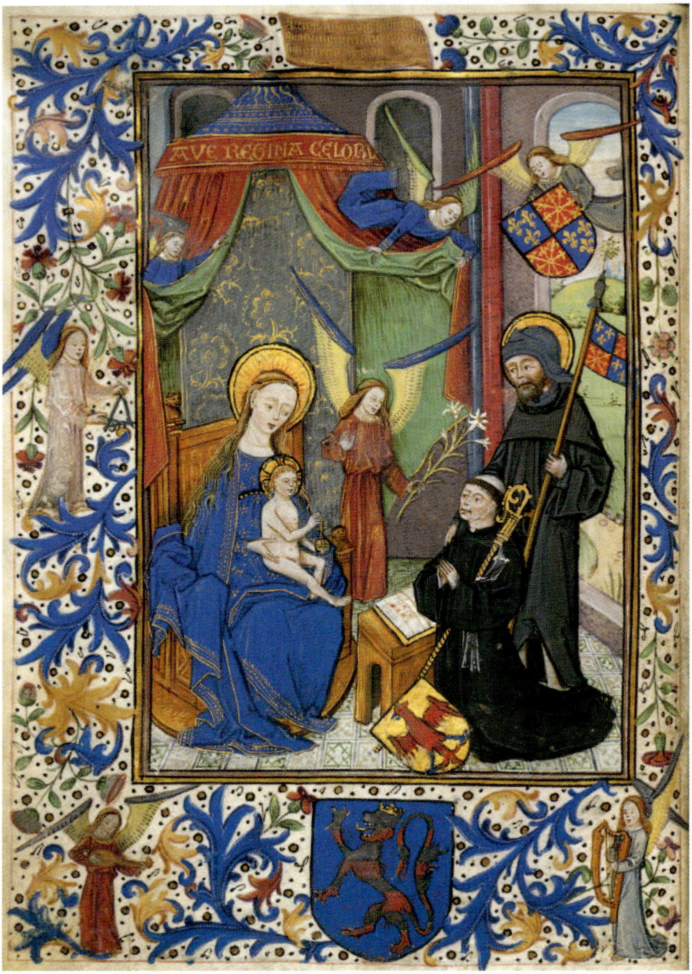

81 *Willem van Bossuyt kneeling before the Virgin and Child*
Missal for the use of the Abbey of St Bavon, Ghent
Ghent, 1483
290 × 200 mm
Add. MS 17440, f. 13v

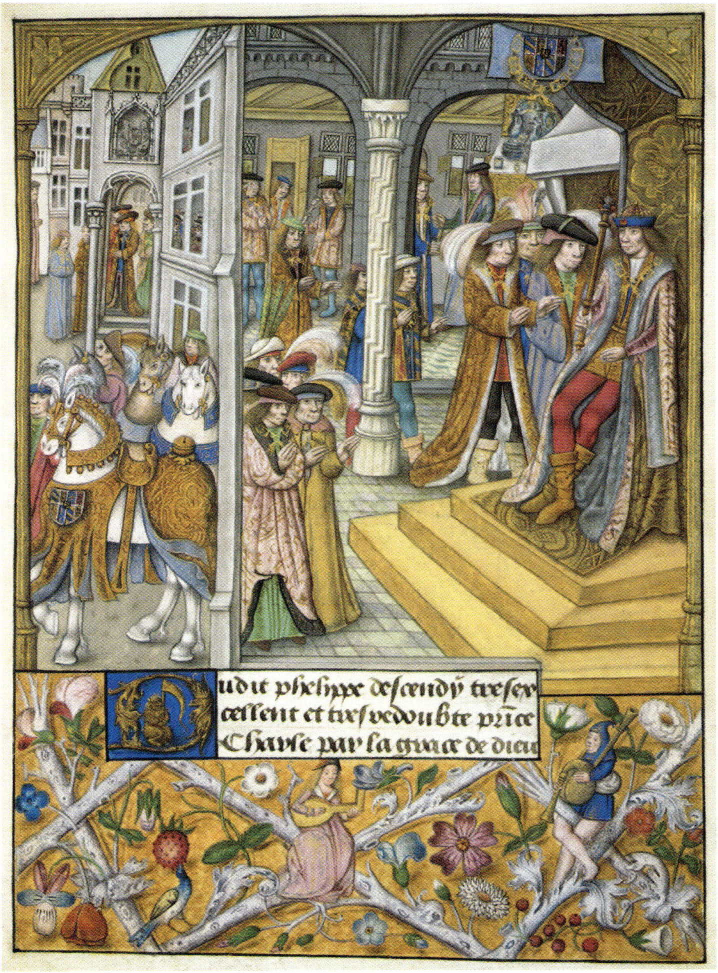

82 *Charles the Bold and his court*
Chroniques abrégées des anciens rois et ducs de Bourgogne
Master of the Trivial Heads
Bruges, c. 1485–1490
230 × 167 mm
Yates Thompson MS 32, f. 14

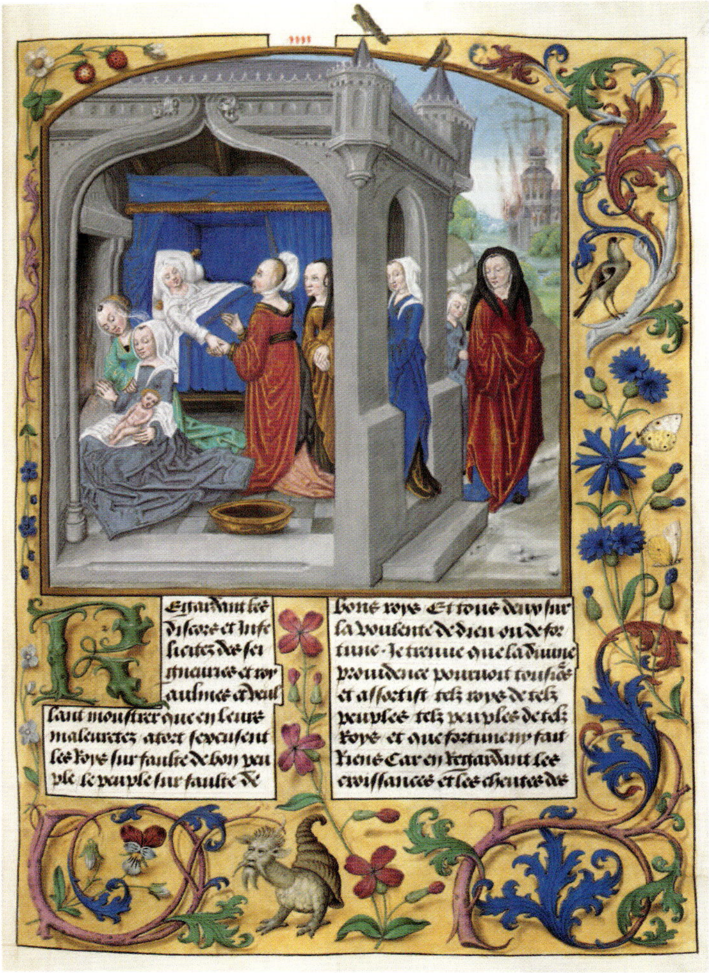

Regardant les
discors et infe
licitez des sei
gneuries et roy
aulmes et veul
lant monstrer que en leurs
maleuretez a tort se veulent
les roys sur faulte de bon peu
ple le peuple sur faulte de
bons roys Et tous deux sur
la voulente de dieu ou de for
tune. Je treuve que la divine
providence pourvoit tousiours
et assortist telz roys de telz
peuples telz peuples de telz
roys et que fortune ny fault
riens Car en regardant les
croissances et les cheutes des

83 *Birth of Alexander the Great*
Quintus Curtius Rufus, *Historia Alexandri magni*.
French translation by Vasco da Lucena
Master of Edward IV, Bruges, *c.* 1485–1490
380 × 275 mm
Royal MS 20 C.iii, f. 15

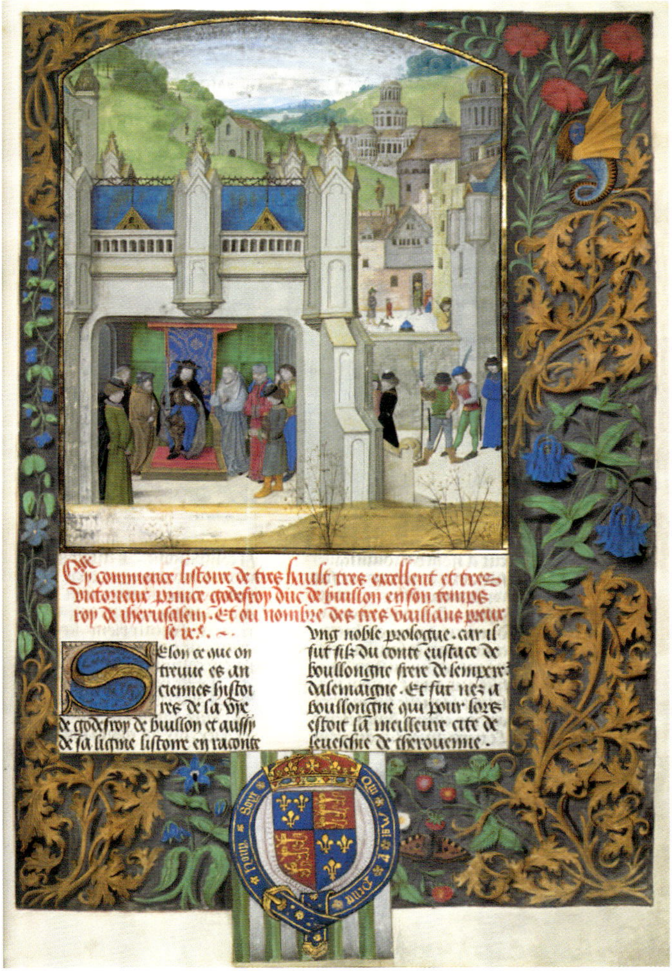

84 *Godfrey of Bouillon in his palace*
Listoire de Godefroy duc de Buillon
Master of the Dresden Prayer book
Bruges, c. 1485–1490
514 × 362 mm
Royal MS 17 F v, f. 3

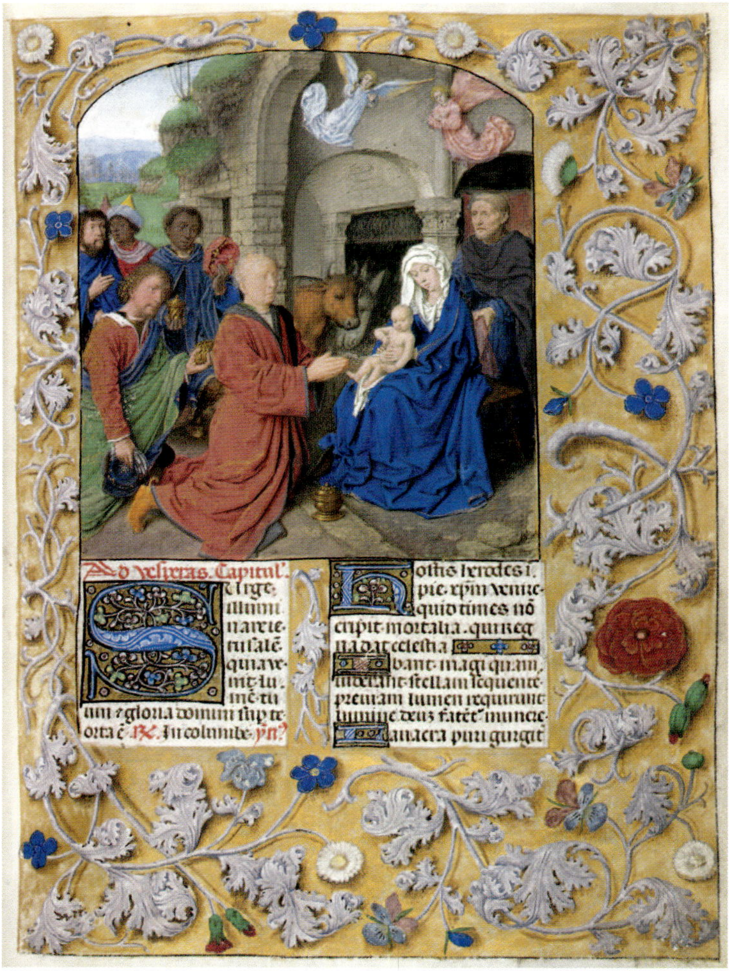

85 *Adoration of the Magi*
Breviary of Isabella of Castile
Gerard David
Bruges, late 1480s
230 × 160 mm
Add. MS 18851, f. 41

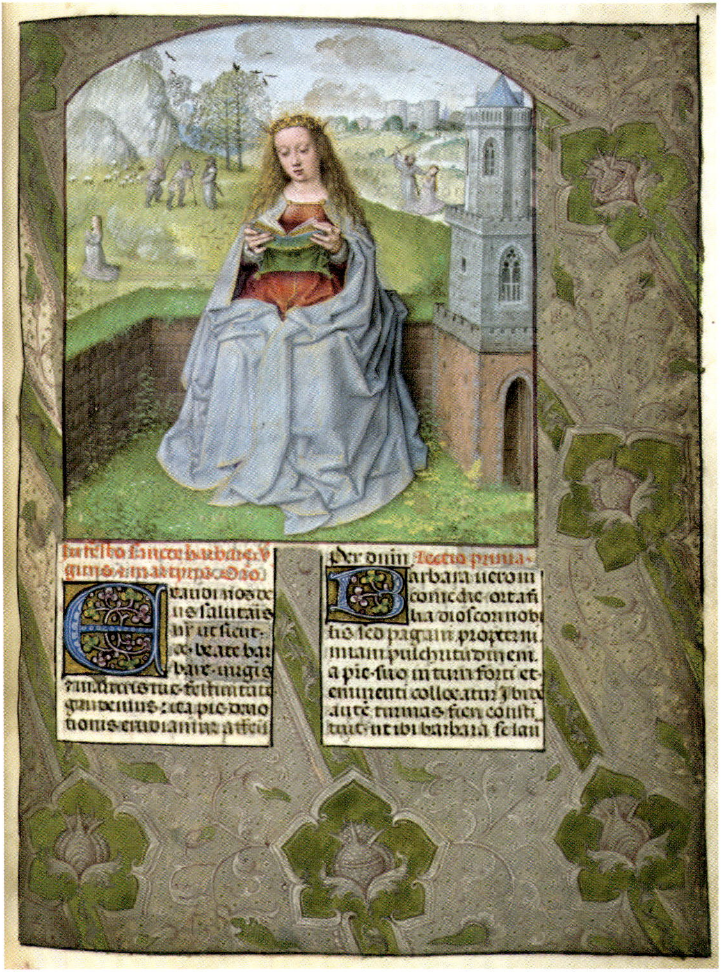

86 *St Barbara*
Breviary of Isabella of Castile
Gerard David
Bruges, before 1497
230 × 160 mm
Add. MS 18851, f. 297

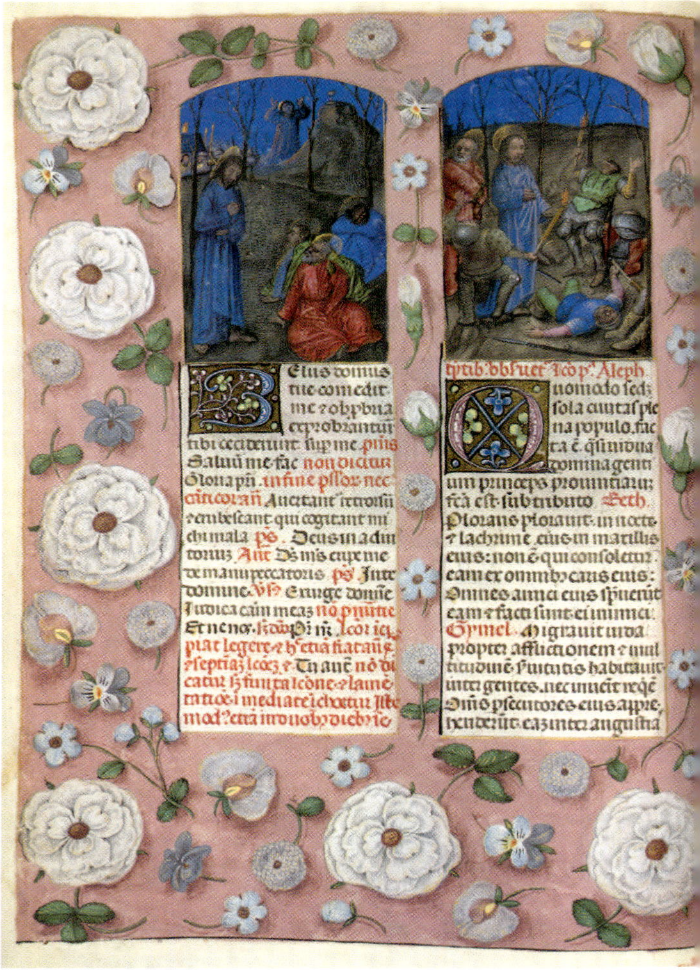

87 & 88 *Agony* and *Arrest; Betrayal* and *Christ before Caiaphas*
Breviary of Isabella of Castile
Master of the Dresden Prayer book
Bruges, late 1480s
230 × 160 mm
Add. MS 18851, ff 100v–101

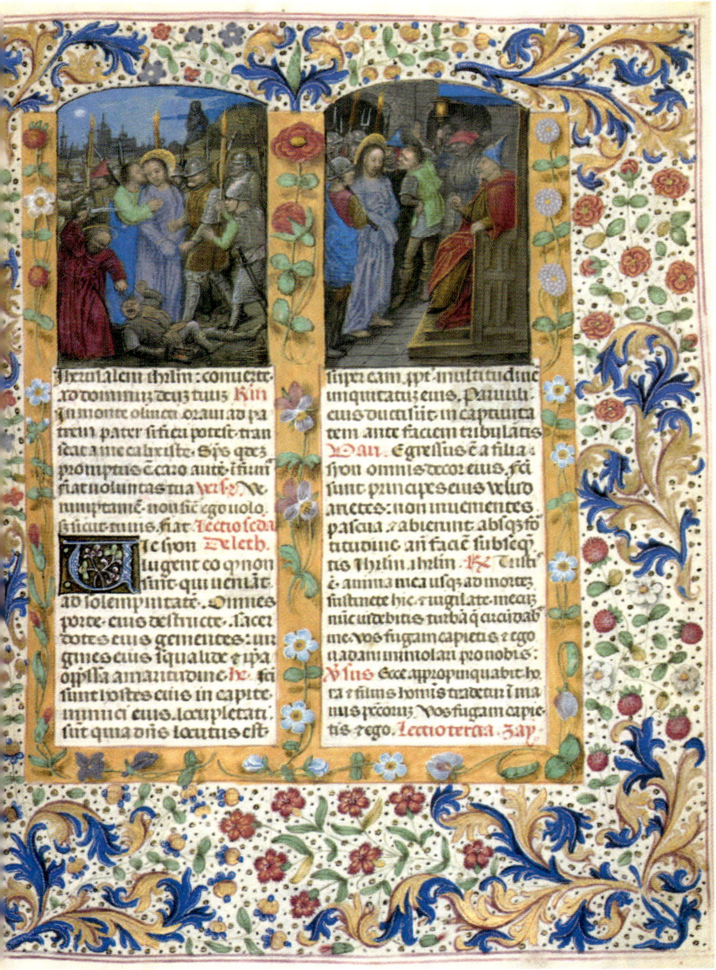

Jherusalem ihrlm: convertere
ad dominum deum tuum. Rñ
In monte oliveti oravi ad pa
trem pater si fieri potest tran
seat a me calix iste. Spiritus quidem
promptus est caro autem infirma
fiat voluntas tua. Vers. Ve
rumptamen non sicut ego volo.
sed sicut tu vis fiat. Lectio secunda
Vie syon Deleth.
lugent eo quod non
sint qui veniant
ad solempnitatem. Omnes
porte eius destructe. Sacer
dotes eius gementes: vir
gines eius squalide et ipsa
oppressa amaritudine. He. Fa
cti sunt hostes eius in capite
inimici eius locupletati
sunt quia dominus locutus est

super eam propter multitudine
iniquitatum eius. Parvuli
eius ducti sunt in captivita
tem ante faciem tribulantis
Vau. Egressus est a filia
syon omnis decor eius. facti
sunt principes eius velud
arietes: non invenientes
pascua et abierunt absque for
titudine ante faciem subsequen
tis. Jhrlm ihrlm. Rñ Tristis
est anima mea usque ad mortem
sustinete hic et vigilate mecum
nunc videbitis turbam que circumdabit
me. Vos fugam capietis et ego
vadam immolari pro vobis.
Versus Ecce appropinquabit ho
ra et filius hominis tradetur in ma
nus peccatorum. Vos fugam capie
tis et ego. Lectio tercia. Zay.

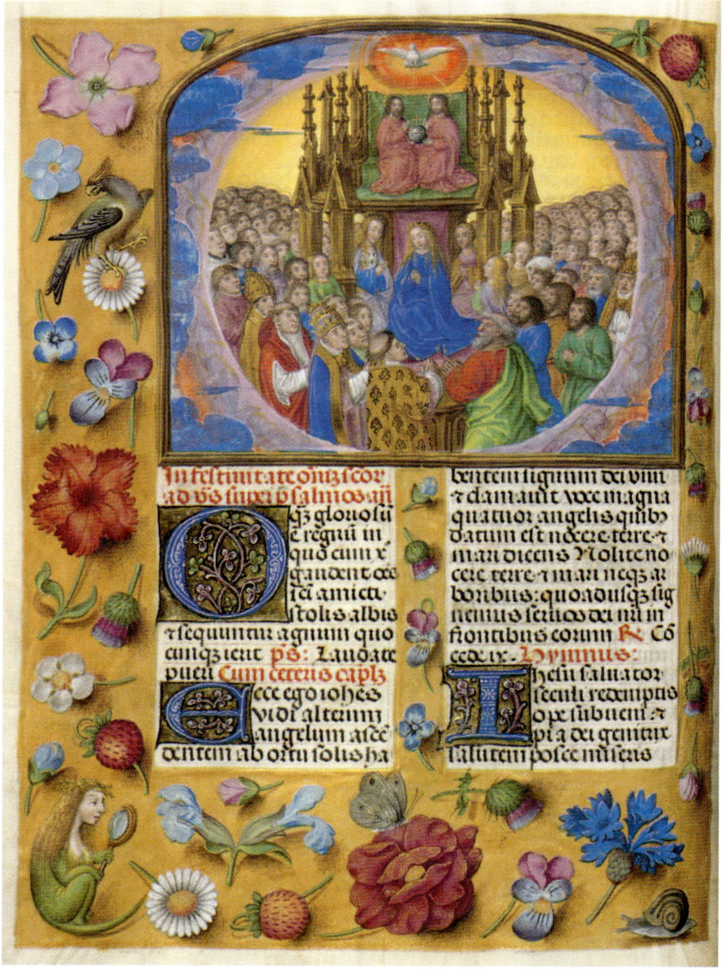

89 *All Saints*
Breviary of Isabella of Castile
Master of James IV of Scotland
Bruges, before 1497
230 × 160 mm
Add. MS 18851, f. 477v

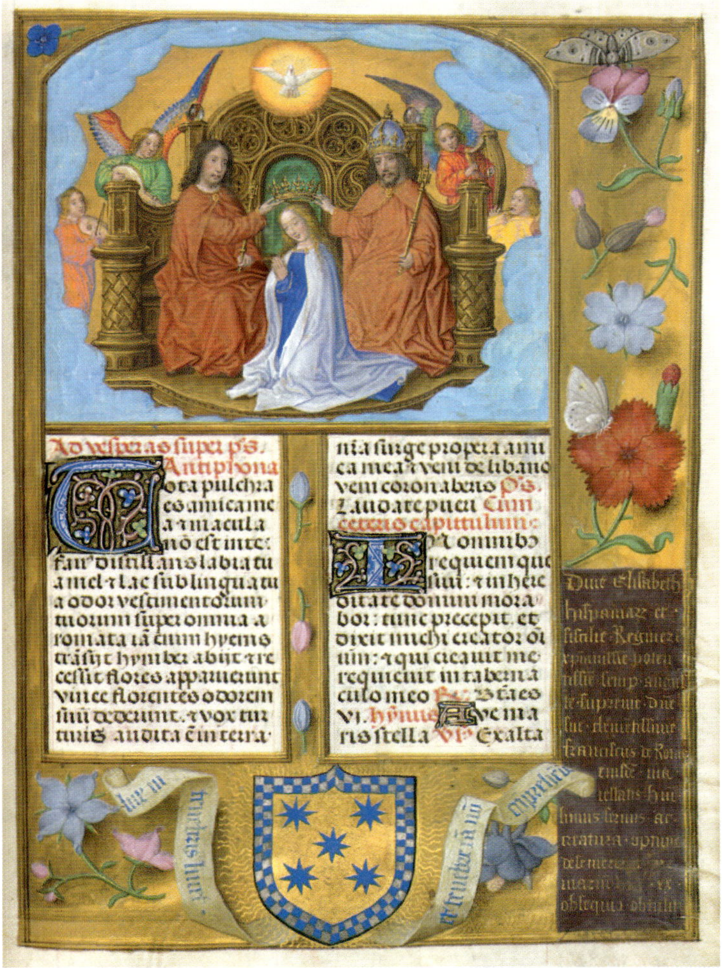

90 Coronation of the Virgin
Breviary of Isabella of Castile
Master of James IV of Scotland
Bruges, before 1497
230 × 160 mm
Add. MS 18851, f. 437

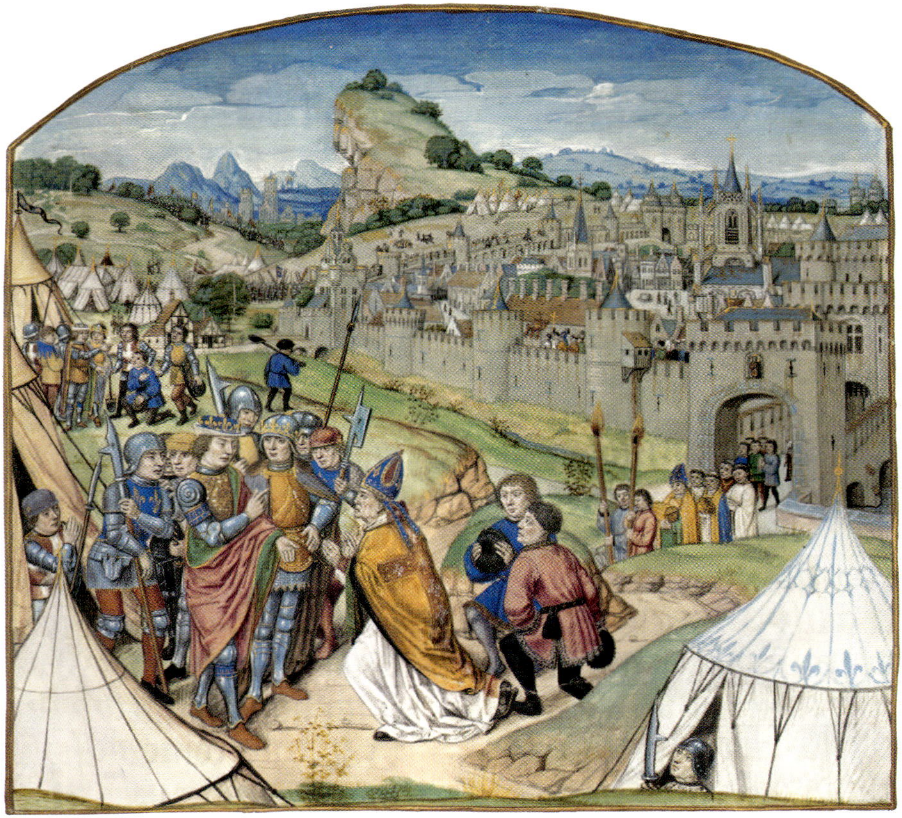

91 *Childebert and Clothaire before Saragossa*
Chroniques de St Denis. Made for Sir Thomas Thwaytes as a gift for Henry VII
Circle of the Master of 1482
Bruges, 1487
525 × 363 mm
Royal MS 20 E I, f. 47 (detail)

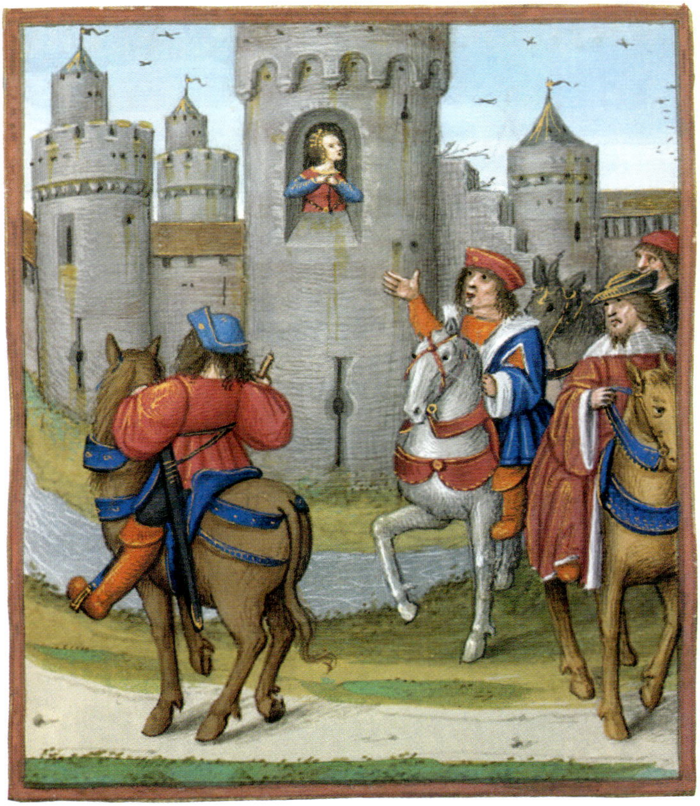

92 *Four knights sent by Britus reaching the Neuf Chastel*
Roman de Perceforest, vol. 2
Circle of the Master of the Prayer books of *c.* 1500
Bruges, *c.* 1490–1500
476 × 353 mm
Royal MS 19 E iii, f. 70 (detail)

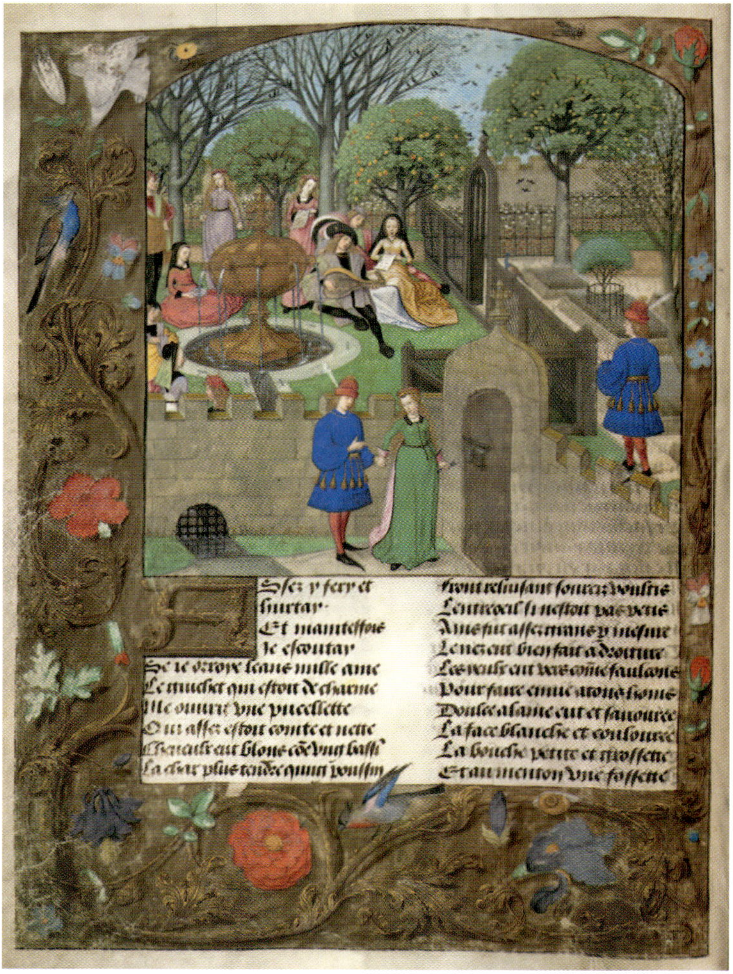

93 Garden of Pleasure

Guillaume de Lorris and Jean de Meun, *Le Roman de la Rose*.
Made for Engelbert II, Count of Nassau and Vianden
Master of the Prayer books of *c.* 1500, Bruges, *c.* 1490–1500
394 × 292 mm
Harley MS 4425, f. 12v

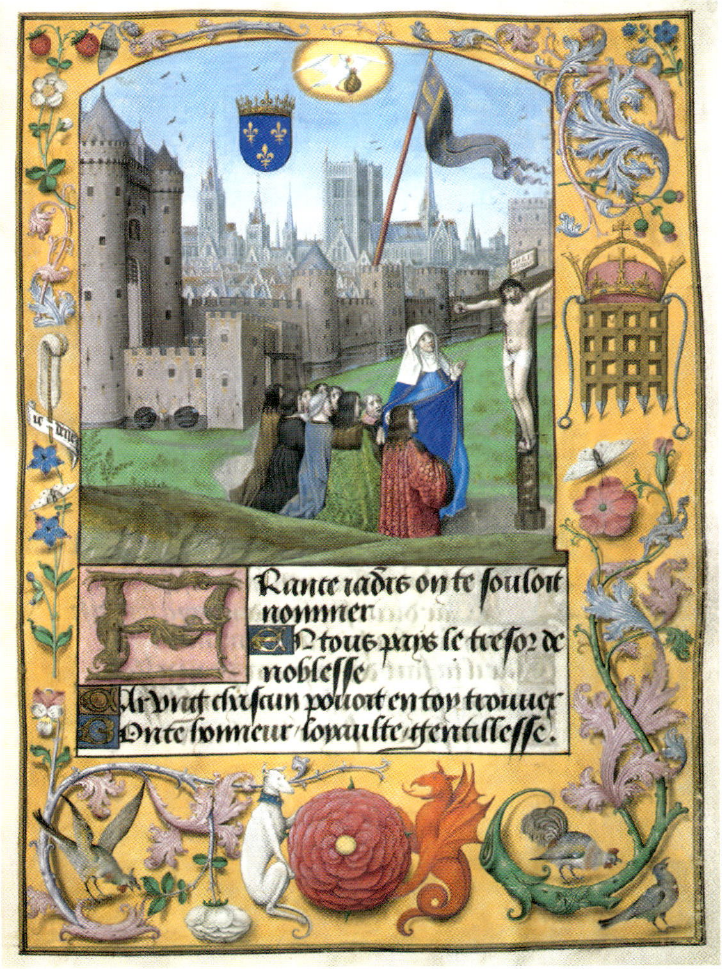

94 *The city of Paris*
Poems of Charles, Duke of Orleans
Master of the Prayer books of *c.* 1500
Bruges, *c.* 1490–1500
375 × 260 mm
Royal MS 16 F ii, f. 89

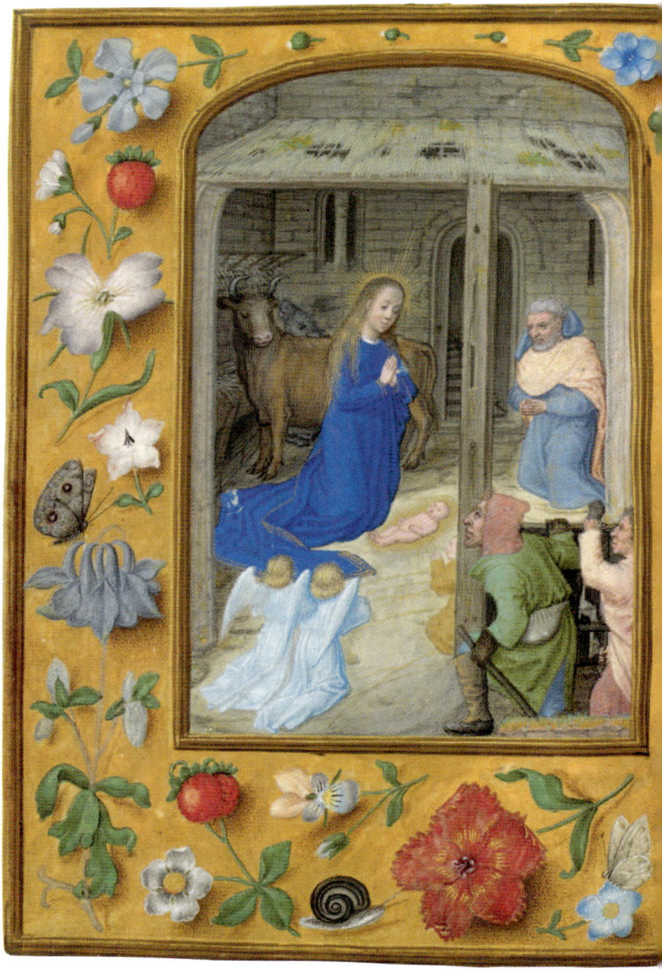

95 & 96 *Nativity* and Prime
Book of Hours, use of Rome
Follower of the Master of the First Prayer book of Maximilian
Bruges, *c.* 1500–1510
158 × 115 mm
Add. MS 35314, ff. 25v-26

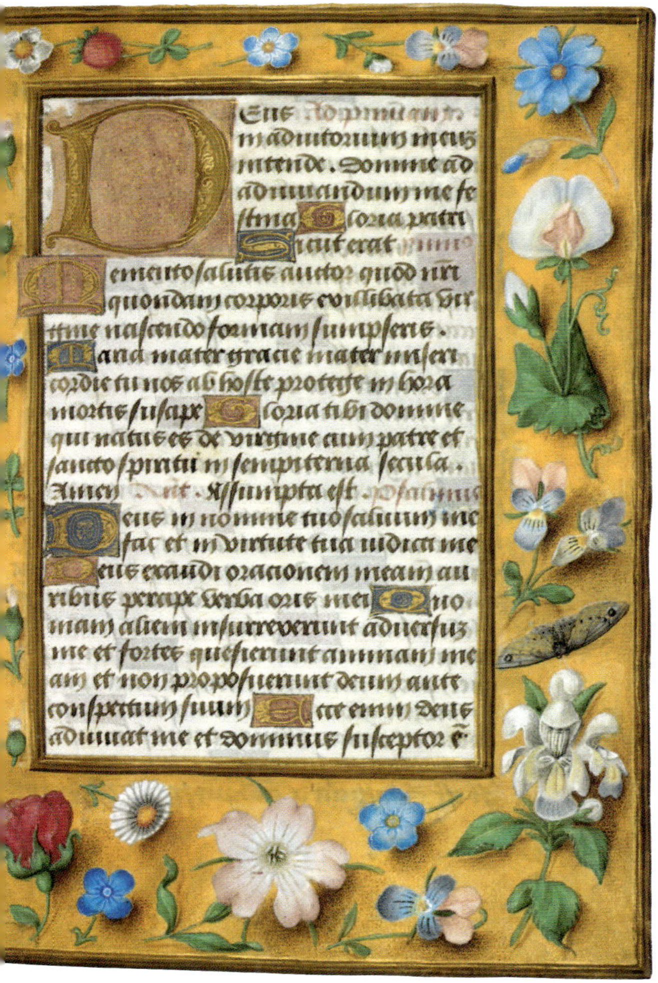
Deus in adiutorium meum intende. Domine ad adiuvandum me festina. Gloria patri. Sicut erat
Memento salutis auctor quod nostri quondam corporis ex illibata virgine nascendo formam sumpseris. Maria mater gratie mater misericordie tu nos ab hoste protege in hora mortis suscipe. Gloria tibi domine qui natus es de virgine cum patre et sancto spiritu in sempiterna secula. Amen. Ant. Assumpta est. Psalmus
Deus in nomine tuo salvum me fac et in virtute tua iudica me. Deus exaudi orationem meam auribus percipe verba oris mei. Quoniam alieni insurrexerunt adversum me et fortes quesierunt animam meam et non proposuerunt deum ante conspectum suum. Ecce enim deus adiuvat me et dominus susceptor est

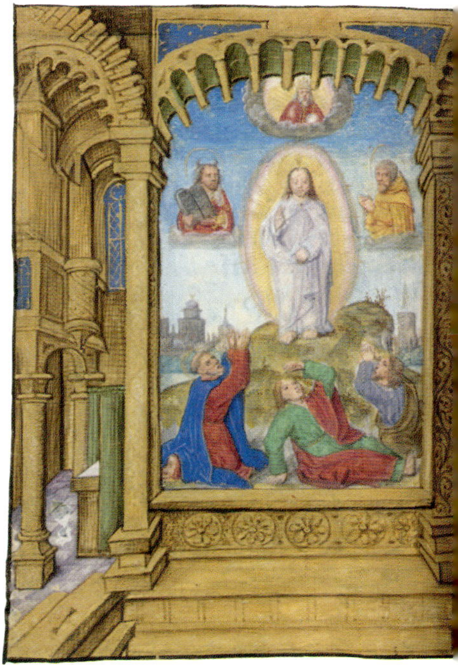

97 & 98 *Transfiguration*
Hours of Joanna of Castile
Master of the David Scenes of the Grimani Breviary
Bruges, between 1496 and 1506
109 × 75 mm
Add. MS 18852, ff. 39v-40 (actual size)

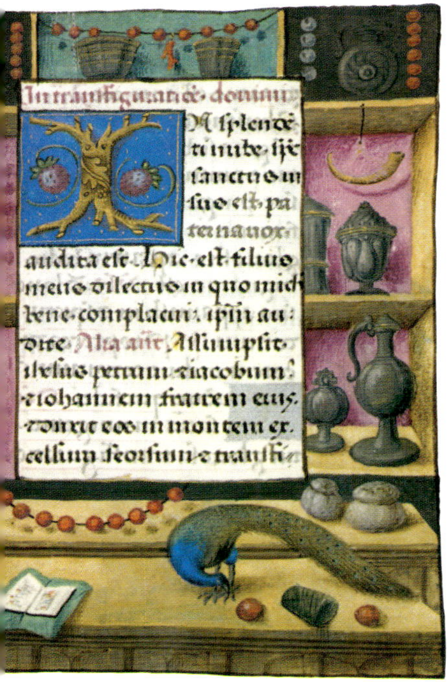
In transfiguratione domini
IN splendenti nube spiritus
sanctus vi
sus est pa
terna uox
audita est· Hic· est filius
meus dilectus in quo michi
bene complacui· ipsum au
dite· Alia añt· Assumpsit
ihesus petrum· et iacobum
et iohannem fratrem eius·
et duxit eos in montem ex
cellum seorsum et transfi

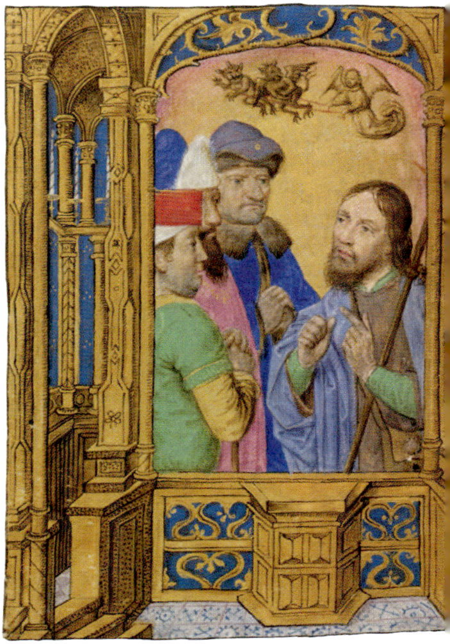

99 & 100 St James the Greater
Hours of Joanna of Castile
Master of the David Scenes of the Grimani Breviary
Bruges, between 1496 and 1506
109 × 75 mm
Add. MS 18852, ff. 411v-412 (actual size)

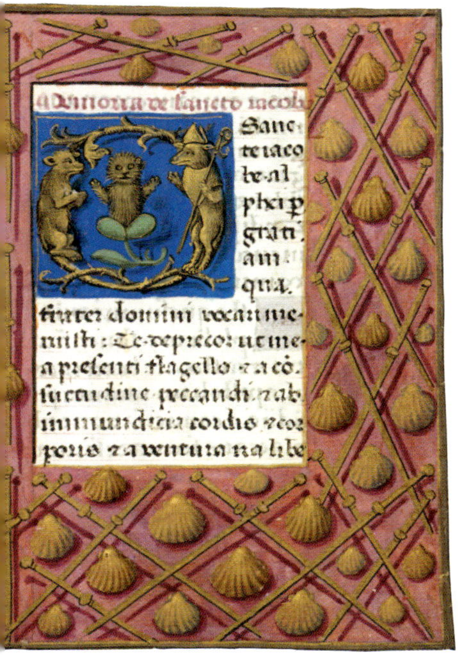
Memoria de sancto iacob
Sanc-
te iaco
be al
phei p
grati
am
qua.
frater domini vocari me-
ruisti: Te deprecor ut me
a presenti flagello et a cō
suetudine peccandi et ab
inmundicia cordis et cor
poris et a ventura ira libe

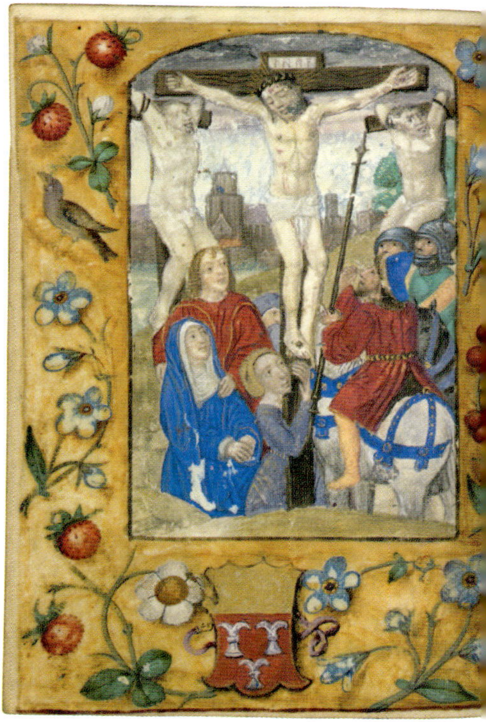

101 & 102 *Crucifixion* and *Arrest*
Hours of Girolamo di Leonardo Frescobaldi and Dionora di Piero Gualterotti
Circle of the Master of the David Scenes of the Grimani Breviary
Bruges, 1490s
98 × 73 mm
Add. 22567, ff. 31v-32 (actual size)

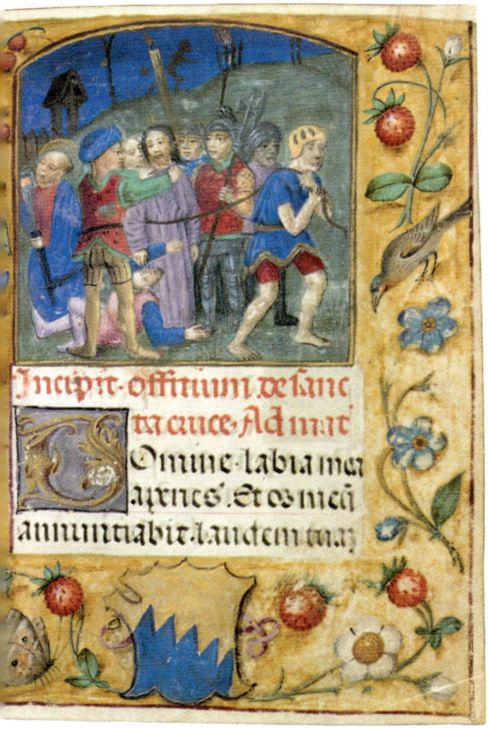
Incipit·offitium de sanc
ta cruce·Ad mat
Omine·labia mea
aperies. Et os meū
annuntiabit laudem tua

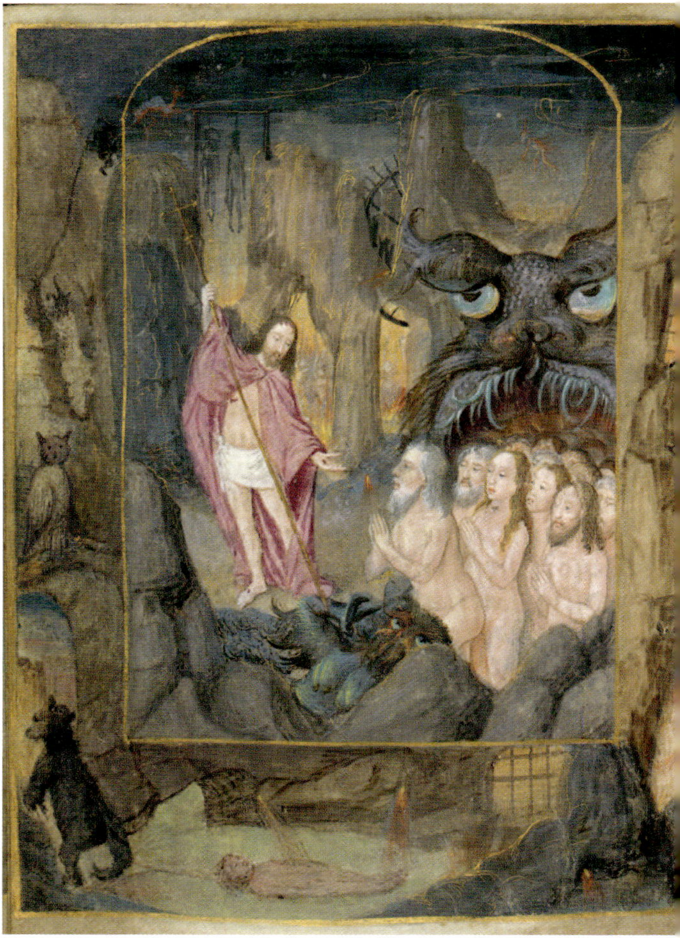

103 & 104 Harrowing of Hell
Vie de Jésus-Christ
Circle of the Master of Antoine Rolin
Valenciennes, *c.* 1500
132 × 97 mm
Add. MS 31838, ff. 42v-43 (actual size)

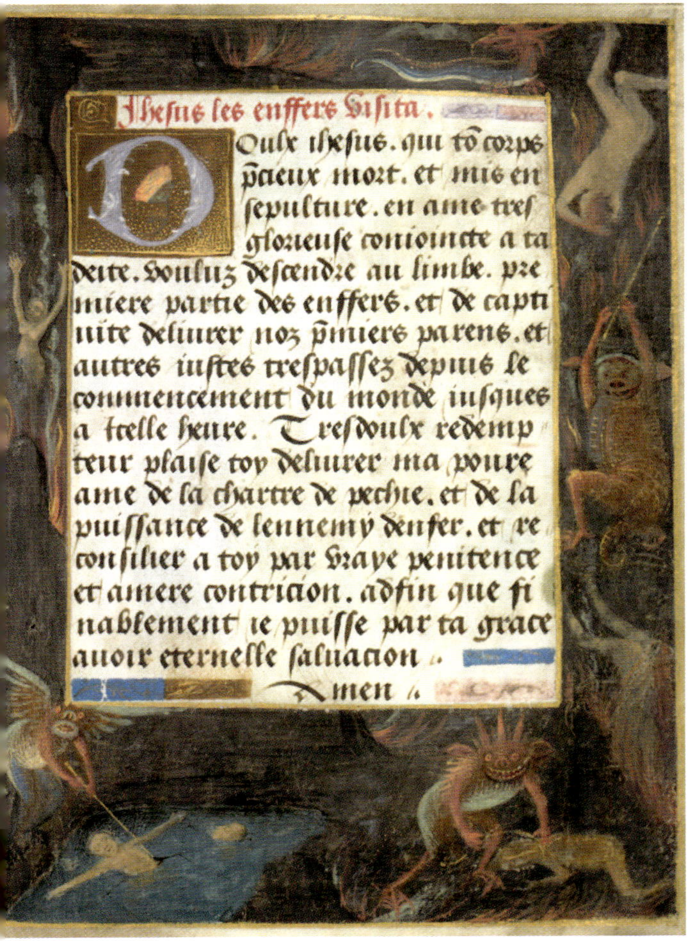
Jhesus les enffers visita.
Doulx ihesus. qui tō corps
p̄cieux mort. et mis en
sepulture. en ame tres
glorieuse conioincte a ta
deite. voulus descendre au limbe. pre
miere partie des enffers. et de capti
uite deliurer noz p̄miers parens. et
autres iustes trespassez depuis le
commencement du monde iusques
a icelle heure. Tresdoulx redemp
teur plaise toy deliurer ma poure
ame de la chartre de pechie. et de la
puissance de lennemy denfer. et re
consilier a toy par vraye penitence
et amere contriction. adfin que fi
nablement ie puisse par ta grace
auoir eternelle saluation.
Amen.

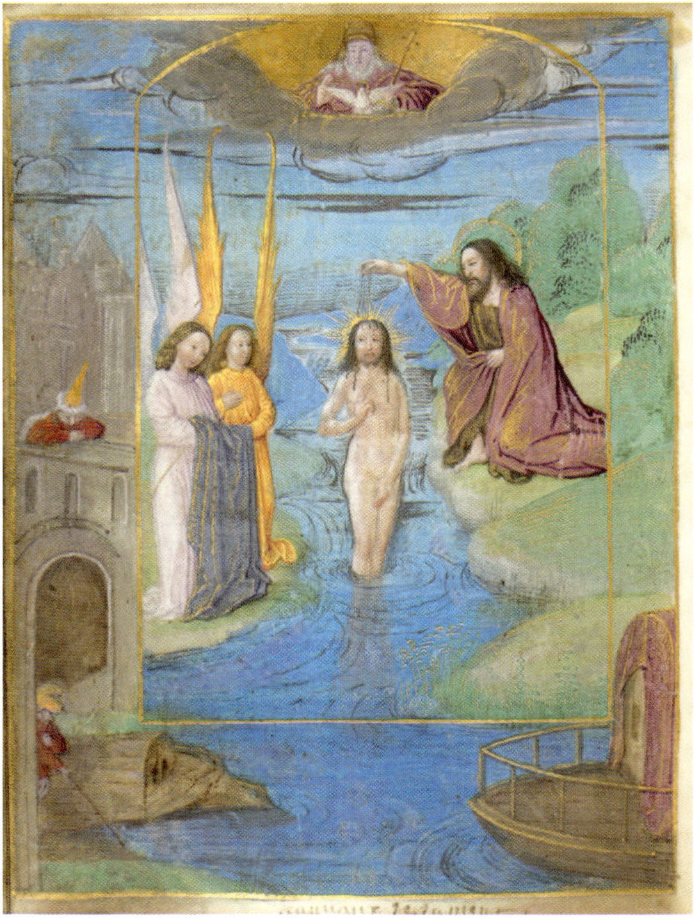

105 *Baptism of Christ*
Vie de Jésus-Christ
Circle of the Master of Antoine Rolin
Valenciennes, *c.* 1500
132 × 97 mm
Add. MS 31838, f. 12v (actual size)

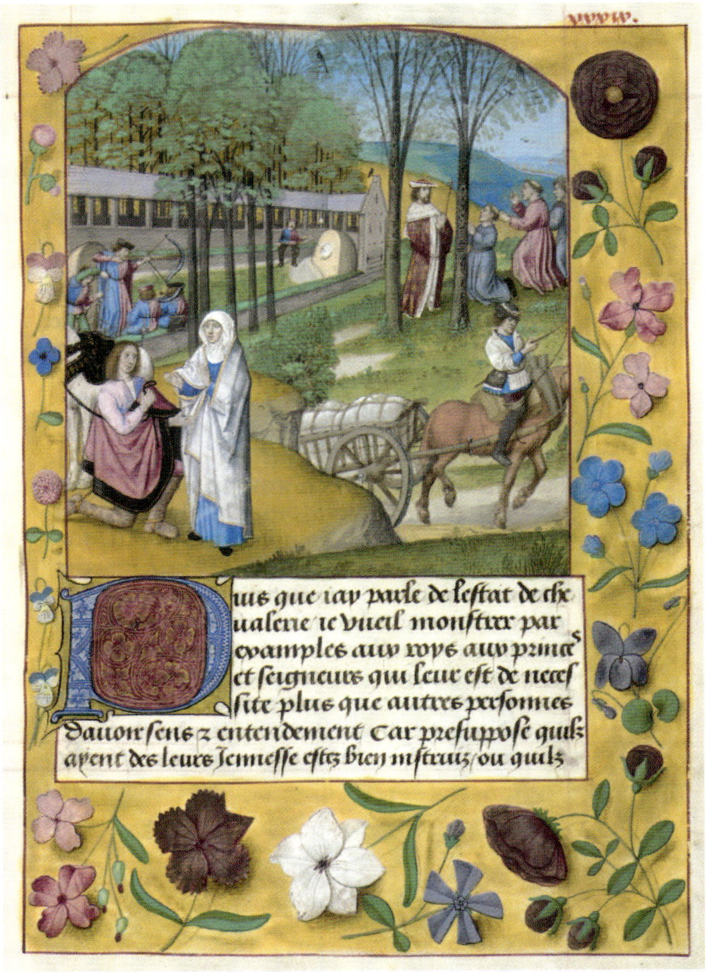

106 *The Archer and Carter as Models for a Prince*
Jean de Lannoy (?), *Imaginacion de la Vraye Noblesse*. Made for Henry VII of England
Master of the Prayer books of *c*. 1500
Sheen, 1496; Bruges, 1496–1497
312 × 215 mm
Royal MS 19 C viii, f. 41

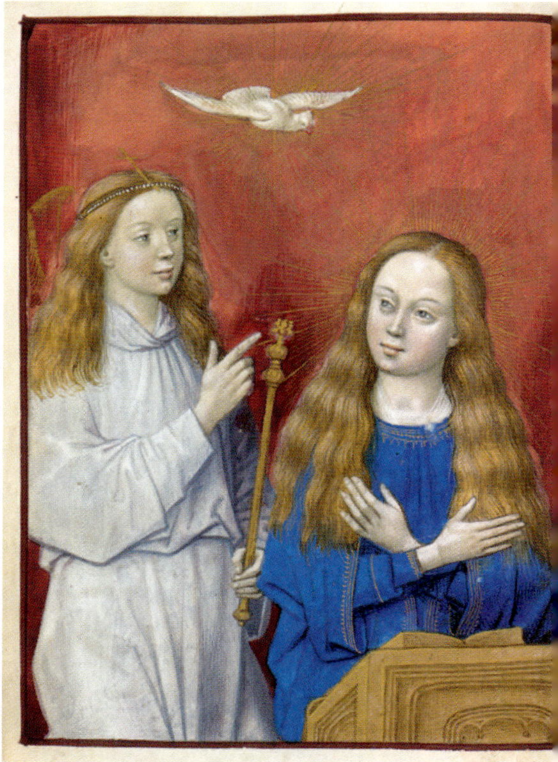

107 & 108 *Annunciation and Tree of Jesse* and Matins
Book of Hours, use of Rome
Master of the Prayer books of *c.* 1500
Bruges, *c.* 1500
135 × 95 mm
Egerton MS 1149, ff. 41v-42 (actual size)

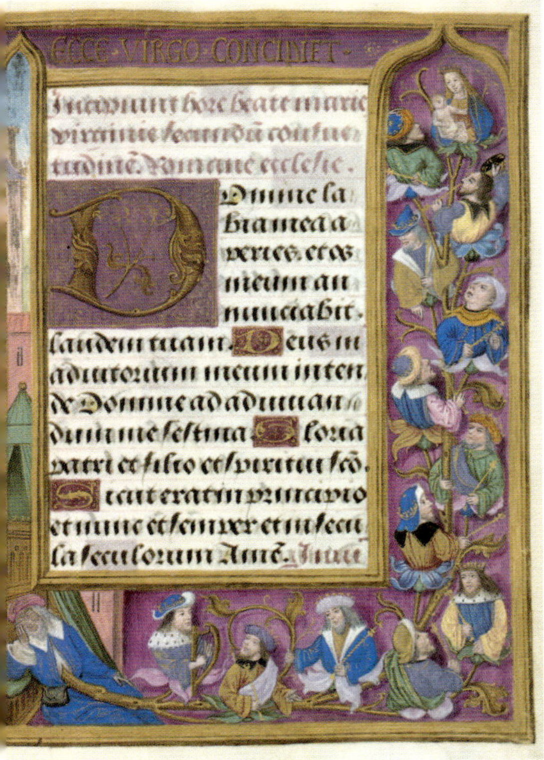
ECCE VIRGO CONCIPIET
Incipiunt hore beate marie
virginis secundum consue-
tudinem Romane ecclesie.
Domine la-
bia mea a-
peries. et os
meum an-
nunciabit.
laudem tuam. Deus in
adiutorium meum inten-
de Domine ad adiuvan-
dum me festina. Gloria
patri et filio et spiritui sancto.
Sicut erat in principio
et nunc et semper et in secu-
la seculorum Amen. Invi

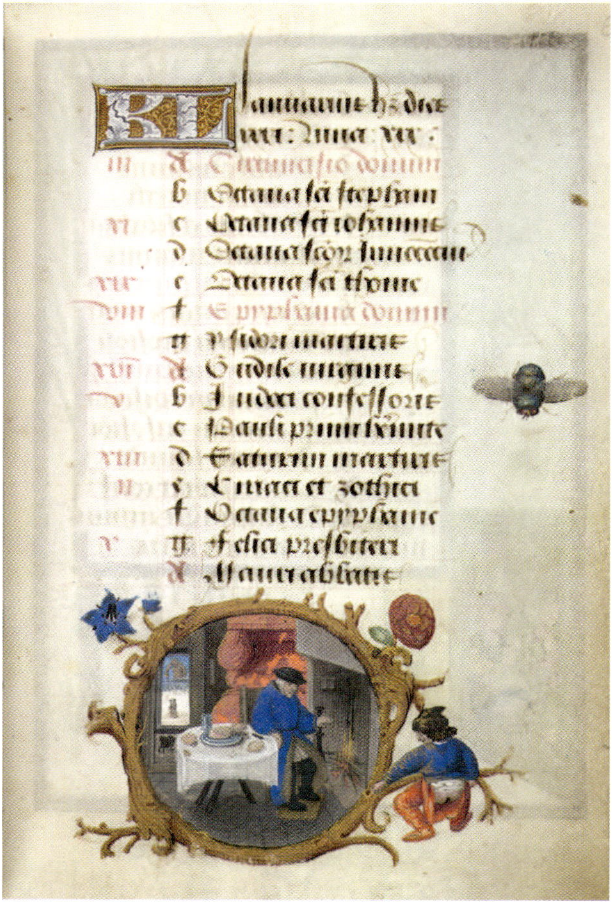

109 *January*
Book of Hours, use of Rome
Master of the Dresden Prayer book
Bruges, *c.* 1500
123 × 83 mm
Egerton MS 1147, f. 6 (actual size)

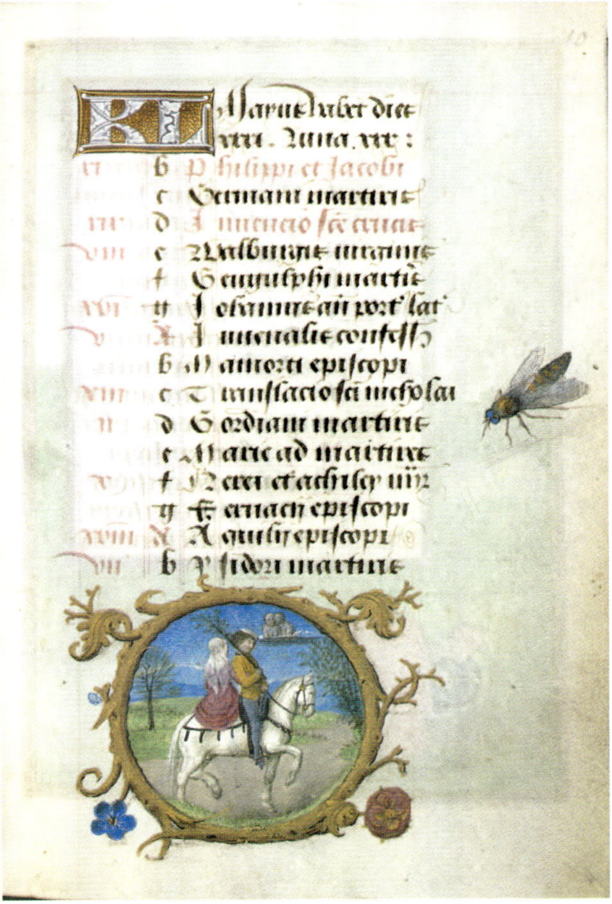

110 May
Book of Hours, use of Rome
Master of the Dresden Prayer book
Bruges, *c.* 1500
123 × 83 mm
Egerton MS 1147, f. 10 (actual size)

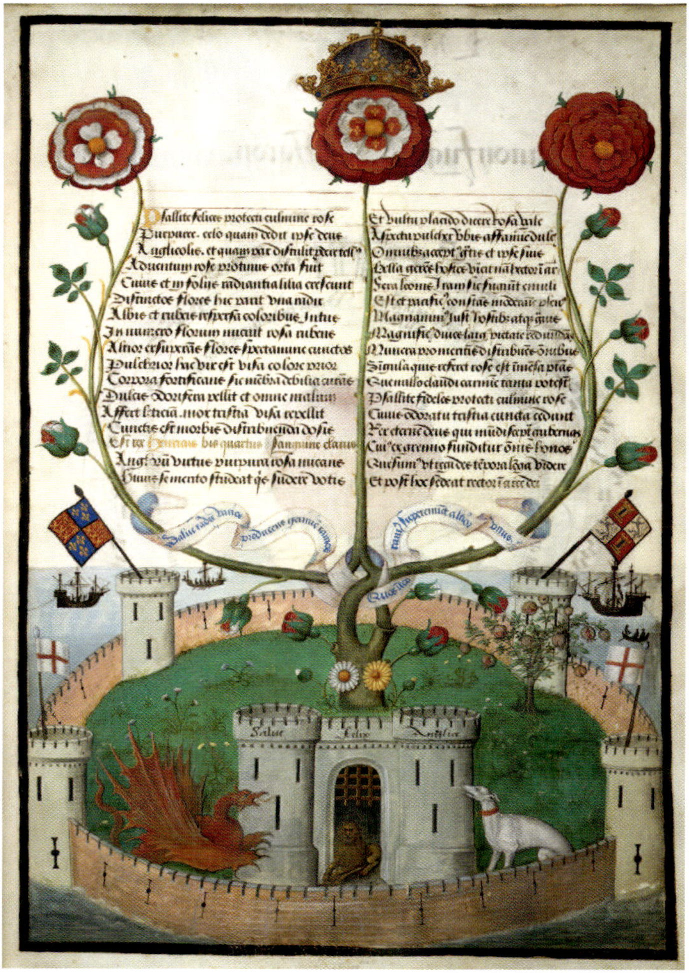

111 *Allegory celebrating the House of Tudor*
Collection of motets by Richard Sampson and Benedictus de Opitiis
London (?), between 1509 and 1516
495 × 345 mm
Royal MS 11 E xi, f. 2

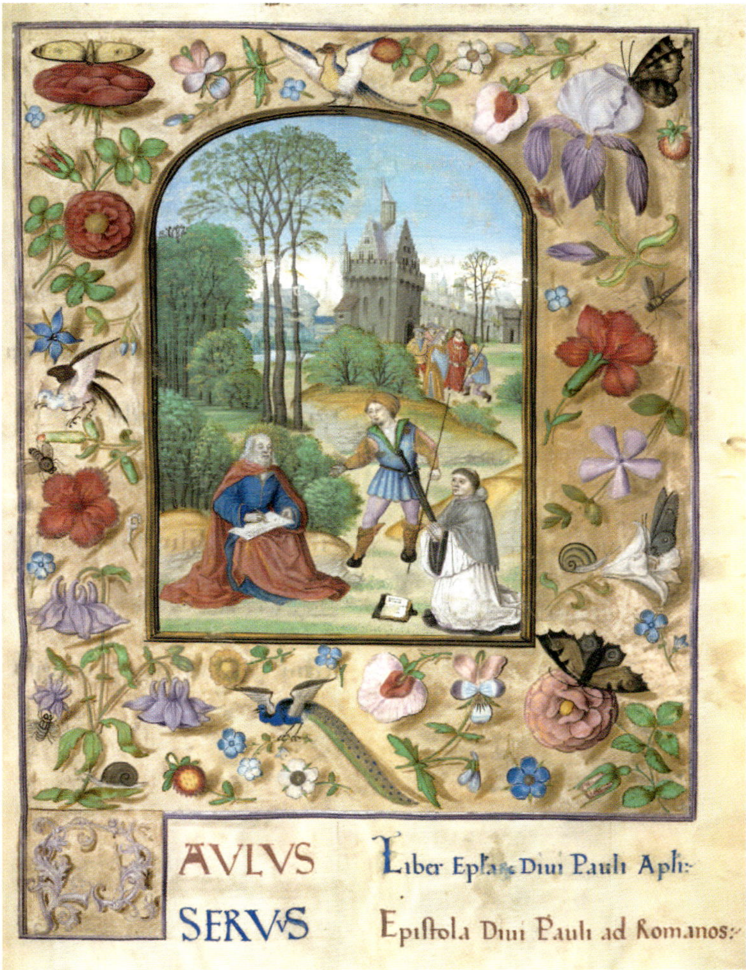

112 *Dean Colet presented to St Paul*
Pauline and Catholic Epistles. Vulgate and translation of Erasmus in parallel.
Made for John Colet, Dean of St Paul's, London
Follower of the Master of the Prayer books of *c.* 1500, London (?), 1506
448 × 303 mm
Royal MS 1 E v, vol. 2, f. 5

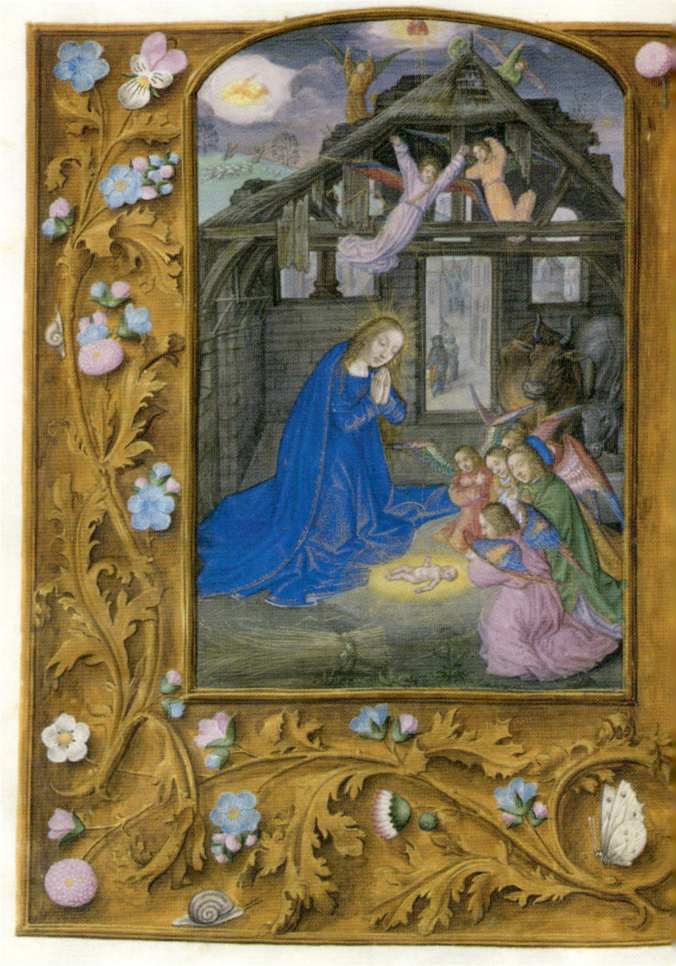

113 & 114 *Nativity* and *Augustus and the Tibyrtine Sibyl*
Book of Hours, use of Rome
Master of James IV of Scotland
Bruges or Ghent, *c.* 1510
237 × 152 mm
Add. MS 35313, ff. 89v-90

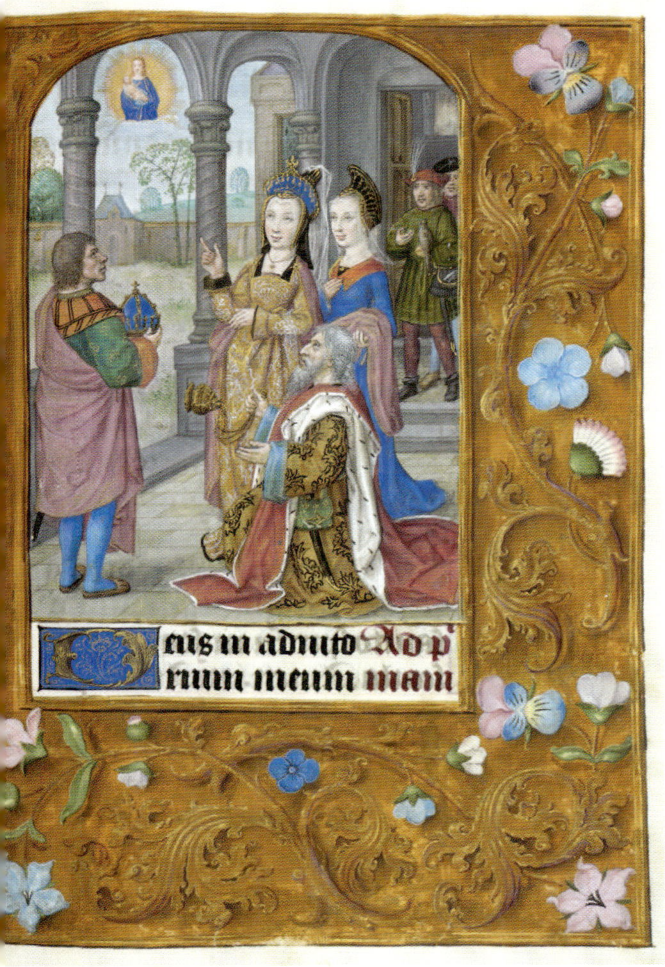
eus in adiuto Ad p'
rium meum mam

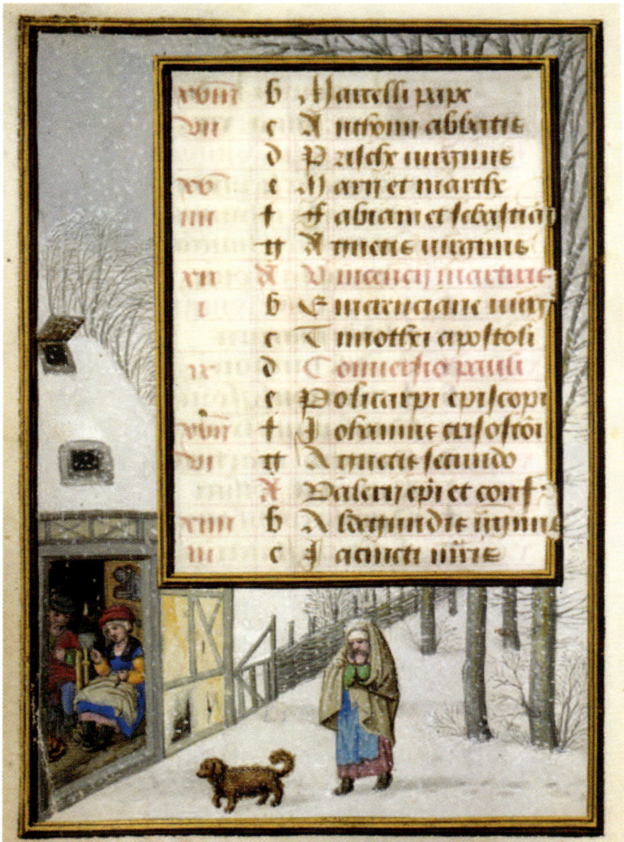

115 *January*
Book of Hours, use of Rome
Simon Bening (?)
Bruges, *c.* 1510–1515
123 × 83 mm
Egerton MS 1147, f. 6v (actual size)

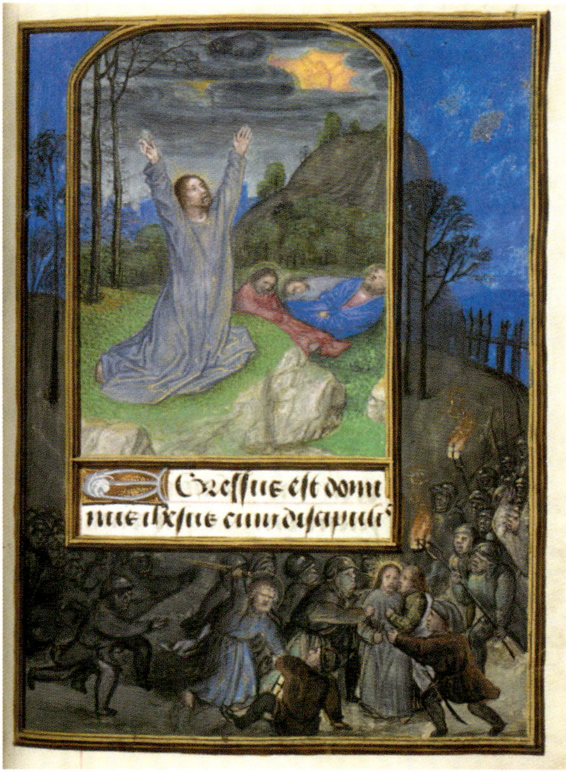

116 *Agony in the Garden and Arrest*
Book of Hours, use of Rome
Simon Bening (?)
Bruges, c. 1510–1515
123 × 83 mm
Egerton MS 1147, f. 229 (actual size)

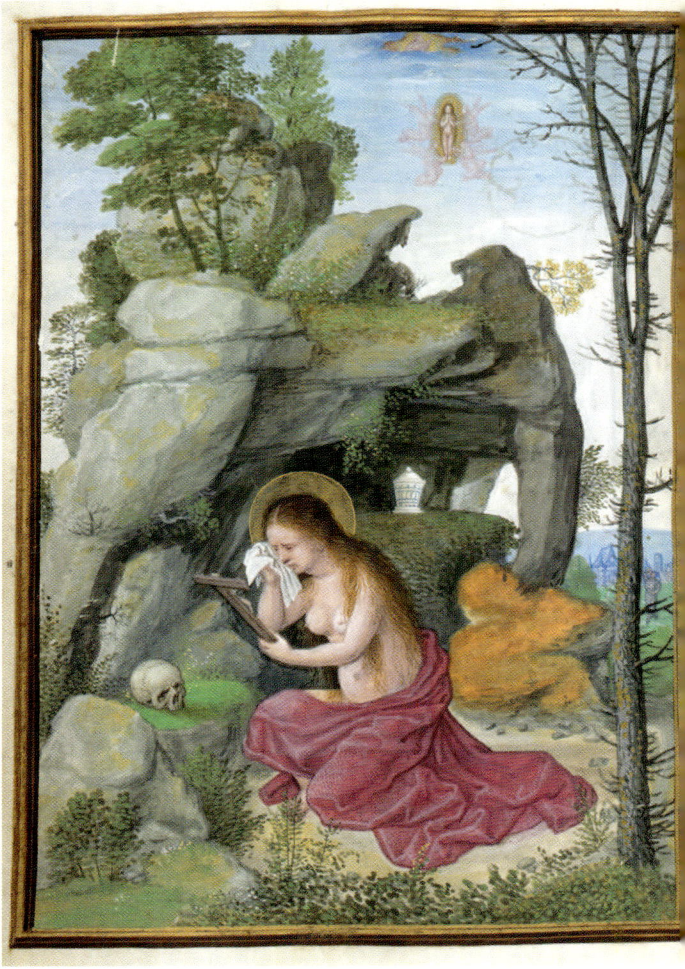

117 & 118 *Mary Magdalen in penitence*
Prayerbook of Joanna of Ghistelles
Simon Bening
Bruges, between 1516 and 1529
150 × 105 mm
Egerton MS 2125, ff. 215v-216

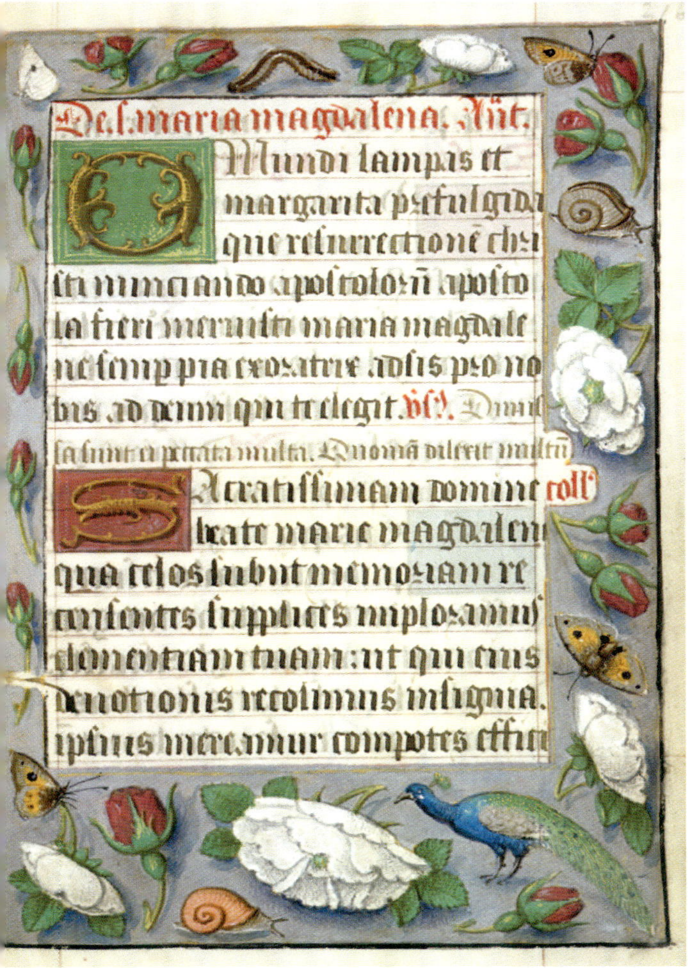
De s. maria magdalena. Ant.
Mundi lampas et
margarita prefulgida
que resurrectionem chri
sti nunciando apostolorum aposto
la fieri meruisti maria magdale
ne semper pia exoratrix adesis pro no
bis ad deum qui te elegit. Vers. Dimit
tuntur ei peccata multa. Quoniam dilexit multum.
Sacratissimam domine Coll.
beate marie magdalene
qua celos subiit memoriam re
colentes supplices imploramus
clementiam tuam: ut qui eius
devotionis recolimus insignia.
ipsius mereamur compotes effici

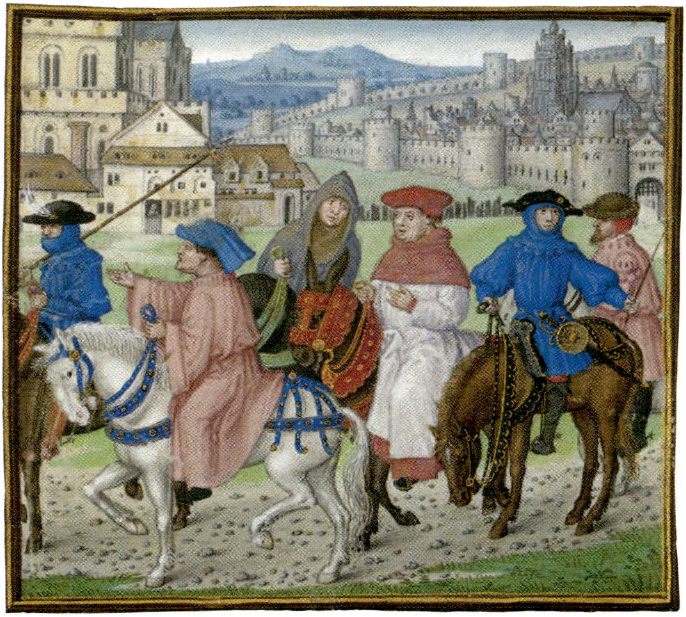

119 *Lydgate and the pilgrims leave Canterbury*
John Lydgate, *Siege of Thebes*
Lucas Horenbout (?)
London (?), *c.* 1525–1530
395 × 280 mm
Royal MS 18 D ii, f. 148 (detail)

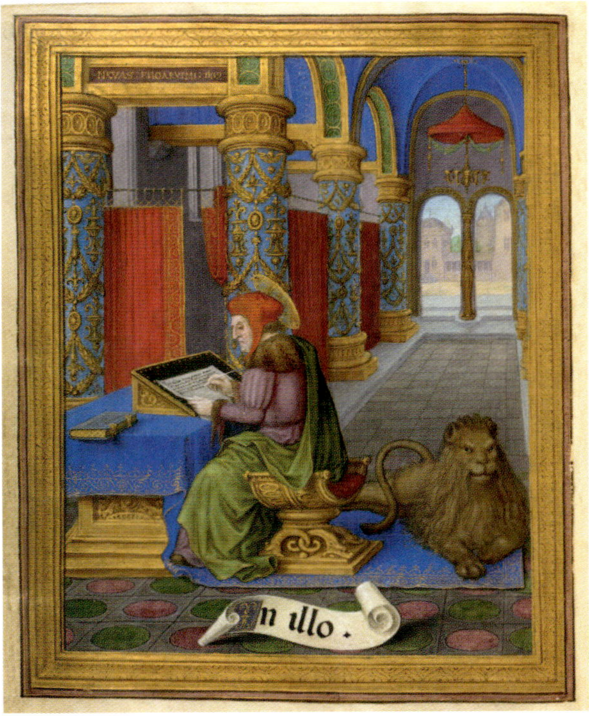

120 St *Mark*
Hours of Bona Sforza
Gerard or Lucas Horenbout
Ghent, c. 1517–1521
130 × 95 mm
Add. MS 34294, f. 10v

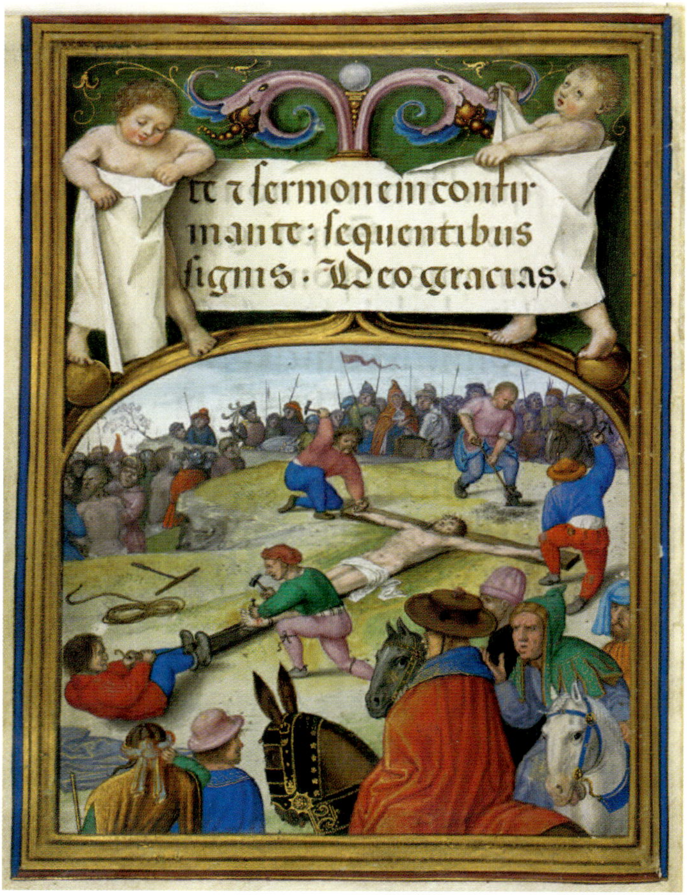

121 *Christ nailed to the Cross*
Hours of Bona Sforza
Gerard or Lucas Horenbout
Ghent, c. 1517–1521
130 × 95 mm
Add. MS 34294, f. 12v (actual size)

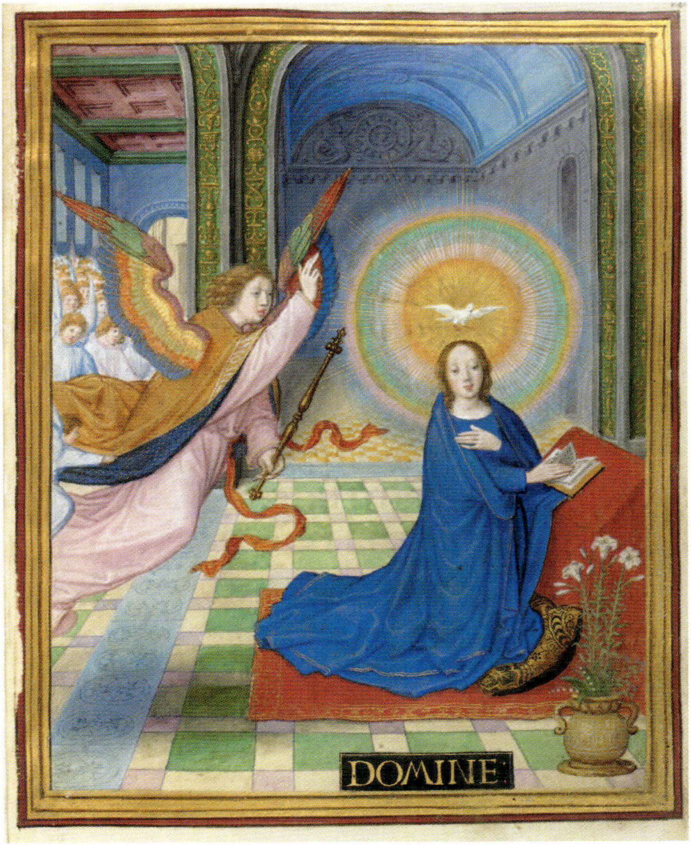

122 *Annunciation*
Hours of Bona Sforza
Gerard or Lucas Horenbout
Ghent, c. 1517–1521
130 × 95 mm
Add. MS 34294, f. 41 (actual size)

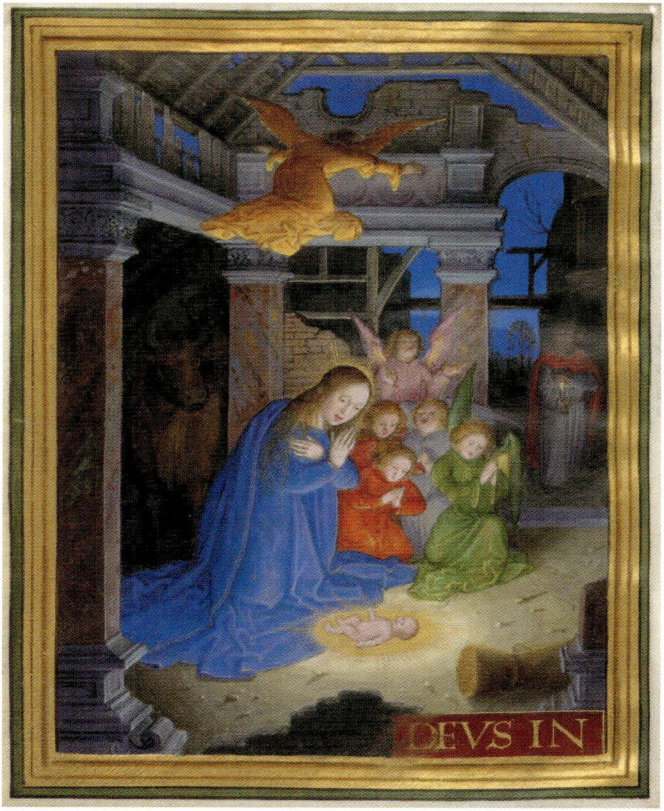

123 Nativity
Hours of Bona Sforza
Gerard or Lucas Horenbout
Ghent, *c.* 1517–1521
130 × 95 mm
Add. MS 34294, f. 82v (actual size)

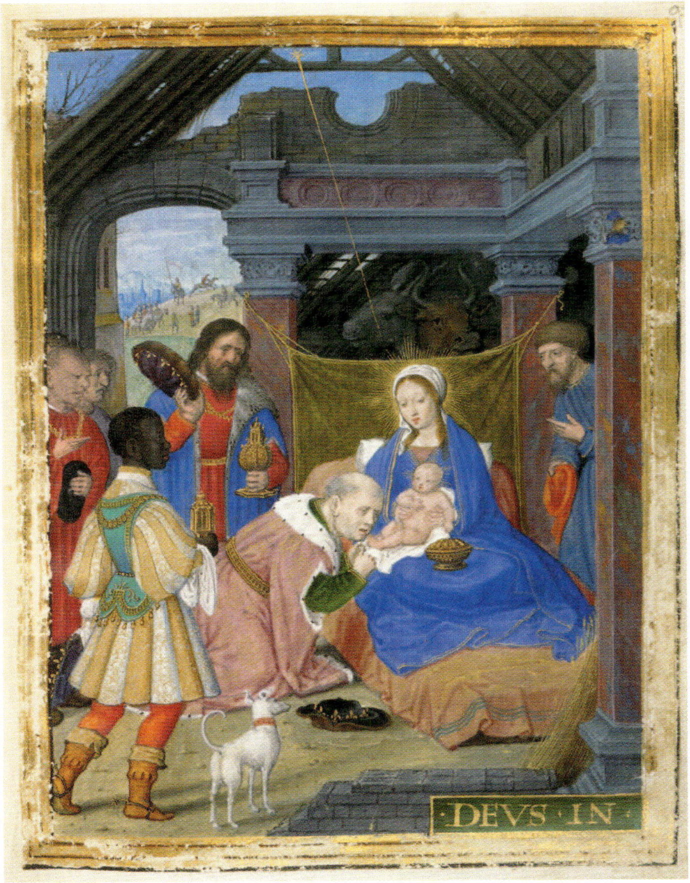

124 *Adoration of the Magi*
Hours of Bona Sforza
Gerard or Lucas Horenbout
Ghent, c. 1517–1521
130 × 95 mm
Add. MS 34294, f. 97 (actual size)

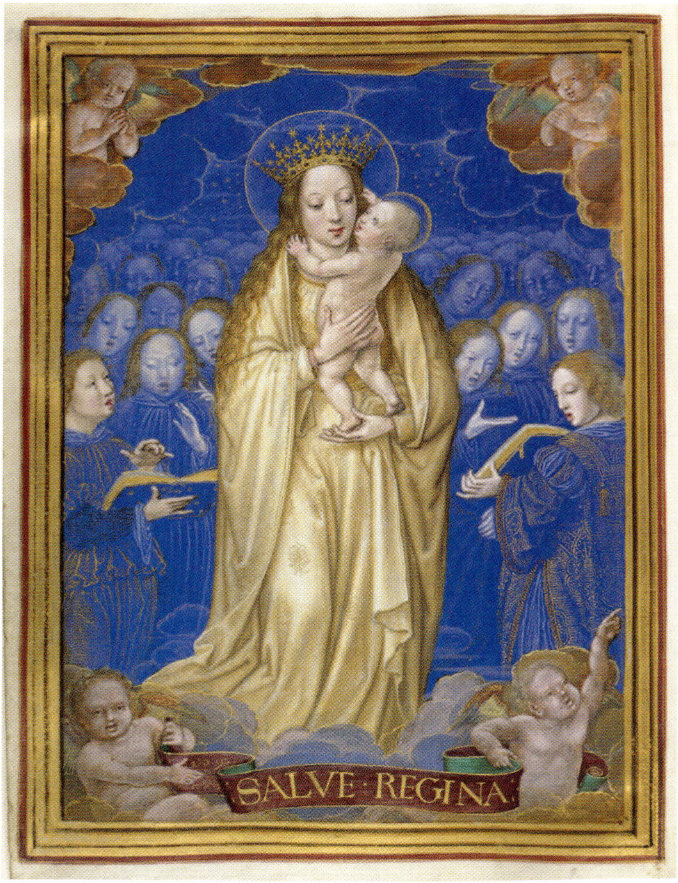

125 *Virgin and Child in Glory*
Hours of Bona Sforza
Gerard or Lucas Horenbout
Ghent, *c.* 1517–1521
130 × 95 mm
Add. MS 34294, f. 133v (actual size)

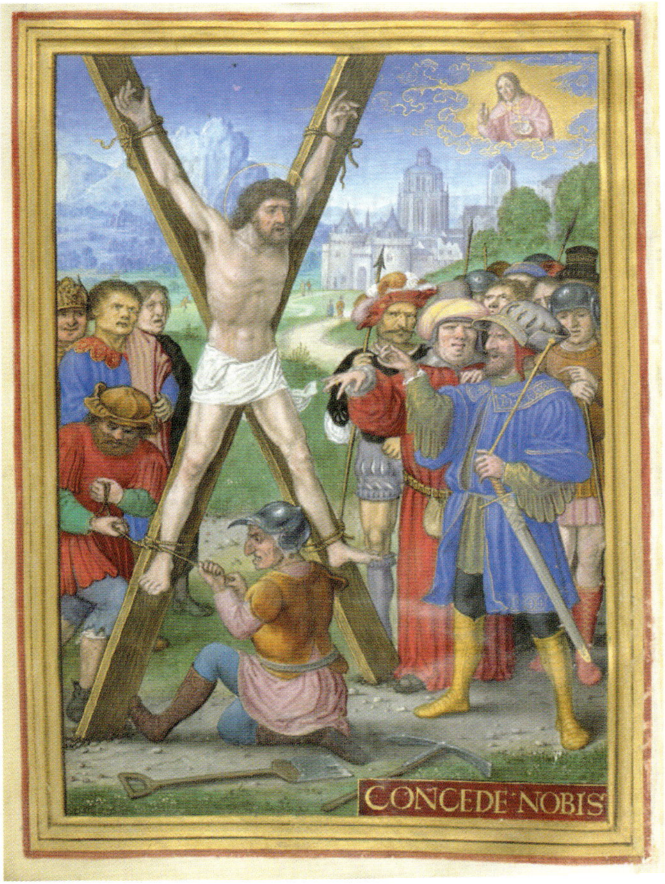

126 *St Andrew*
Hours of Bona Sforza
Gerard or Lucas Horenbout
Ghent, c. 1517–1521
130 × 95 mm
Add. MS 34294, f. 189 (actual size)

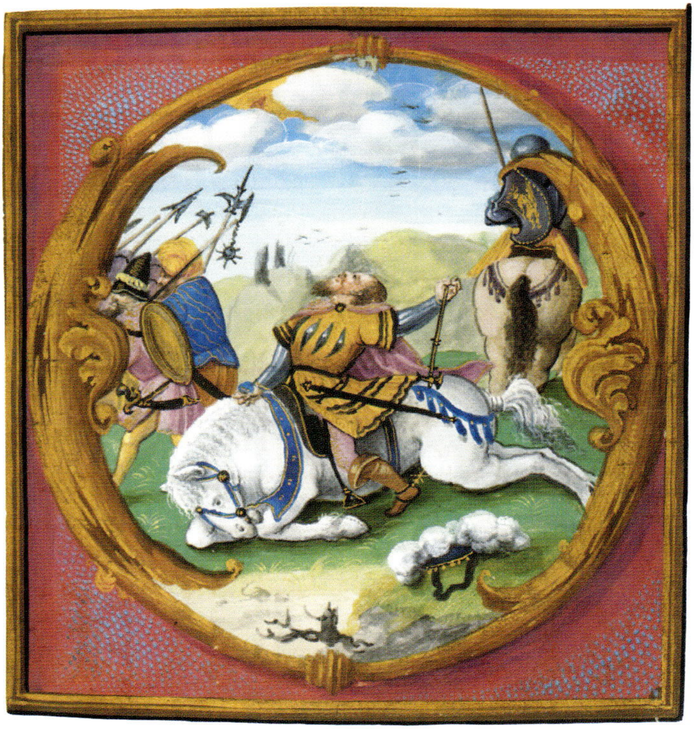

127 *Conversion of St Paul*
Psalter and Antiphonary for the use of the Abbey of Tongerloo
Made for Abbot Antonius Tsgrooten (d. 1530)
Leuven and Antwerp, 1522
600 × 390 mm
Add. MS 15427, f. 277 (detail, actual size)

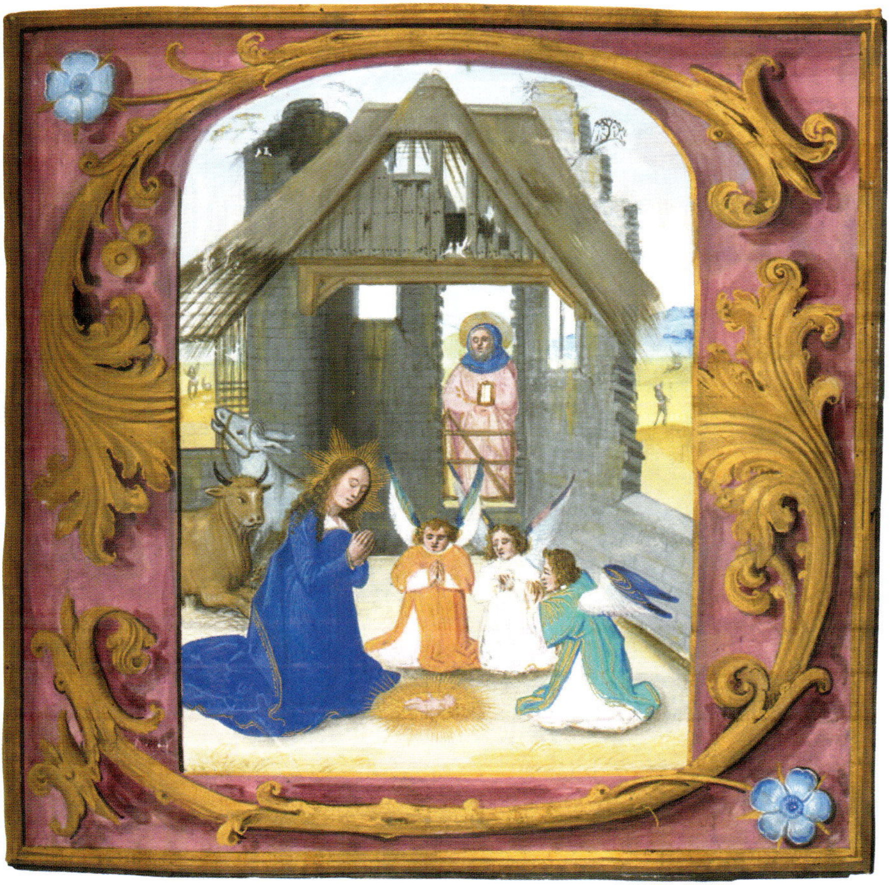

128 *Nativity*
Psalter and Antiphonary for the use of the Abbey of Tongerloo
Made for Abbot Antonius Tsgrooten (d. 1530)
Leuven and Antwerp, 1522
600 × 390 mm
Add. MS 15427, f. 46 (detail)

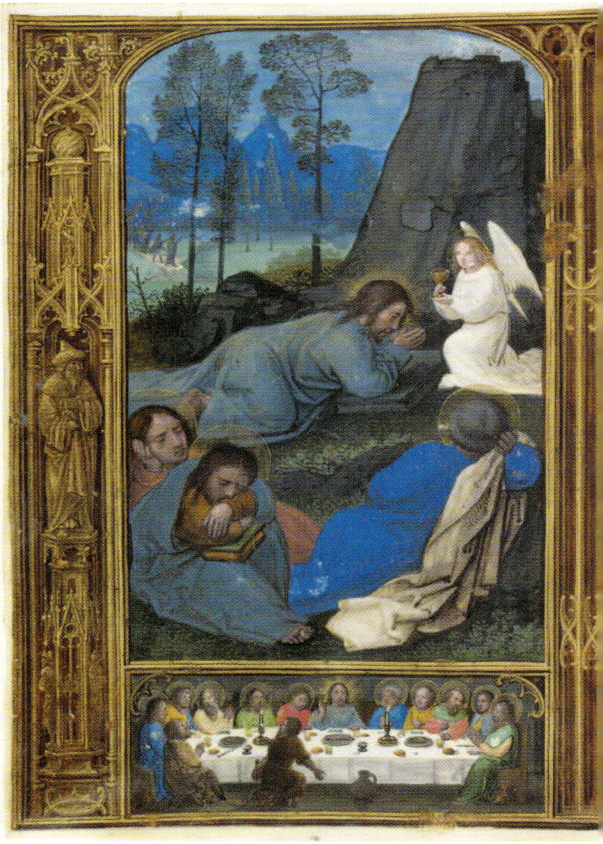

129 & 130 *Agony in the Garden*, *Last Supper* and Matins
Golf Book
Simon Bening and workshop
Bruges, 1530s
115 × 80 mm
Add. MS 24098, ff. 2v-3 (actual size)

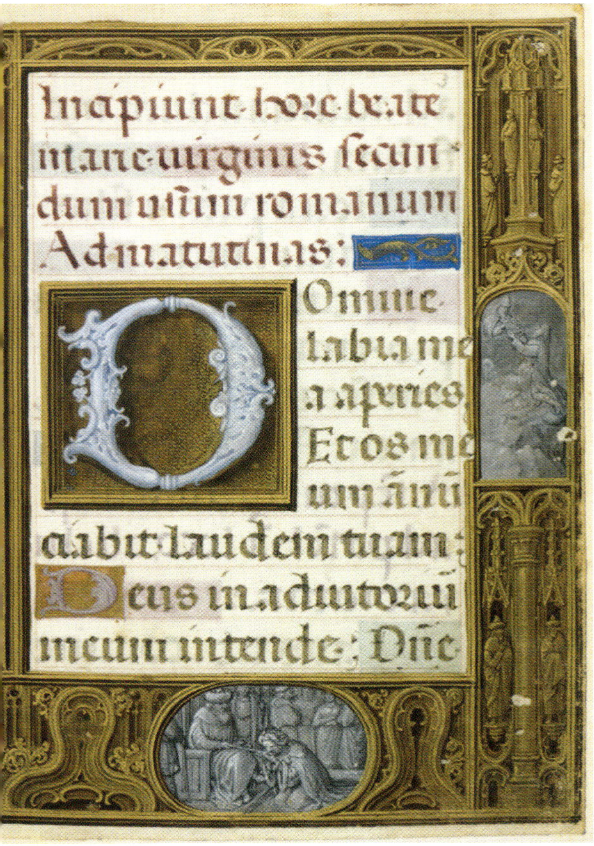
Incipiunt hore beate
marie virginis secun
dum usum romanum
Ad matutinas:
omine
labia me
a aperies.
Et os me
um annũ
ciabit laudem tuam:
Deus in adiutoriũ
meum intende: Dñe

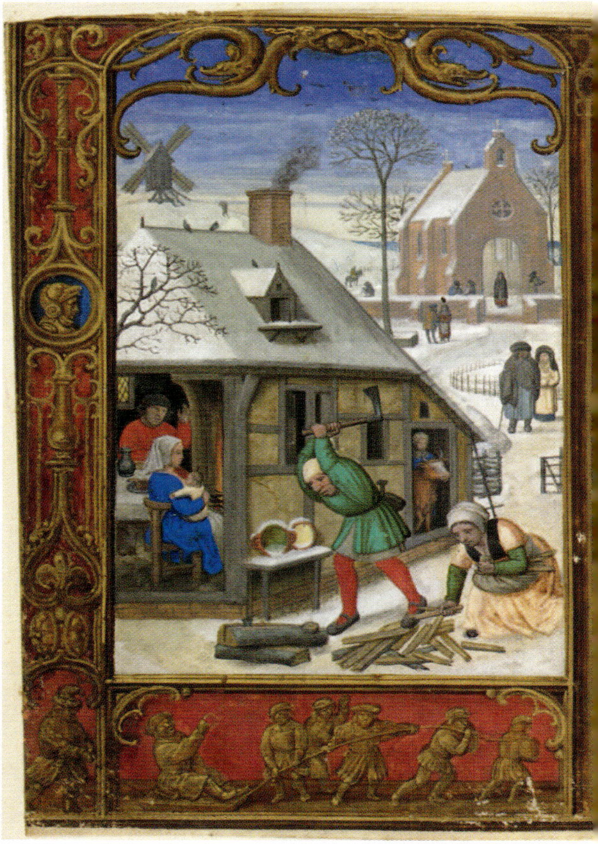

131 & 132 *January*
Golf Book
Simon Bening and workshop
Bruges, 1530s
115 × 80 mm
Add. MS 24098, ff. 18v-19 (actual size)

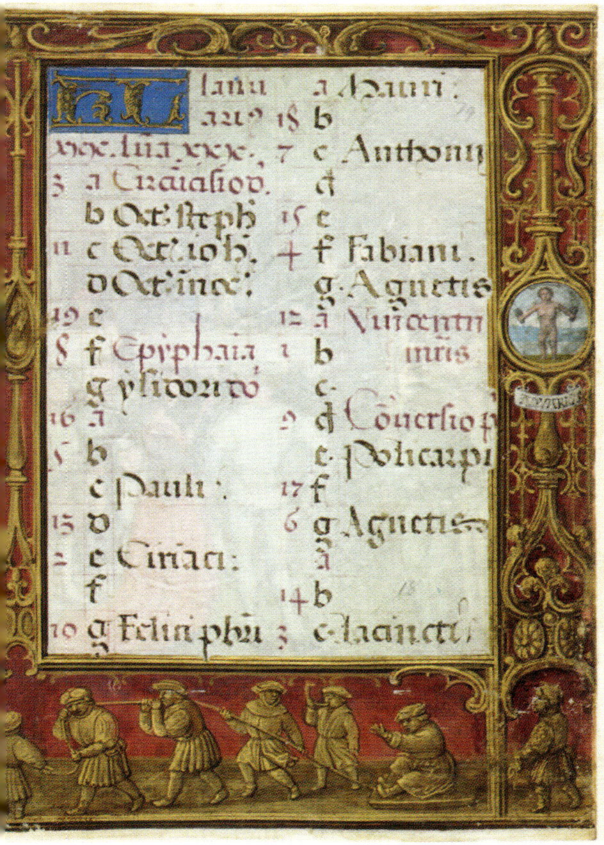
Anthonij
Fabiani.
Agnetis
Epiphania
Conversio p
Policarpi
Pauli
Agnetis

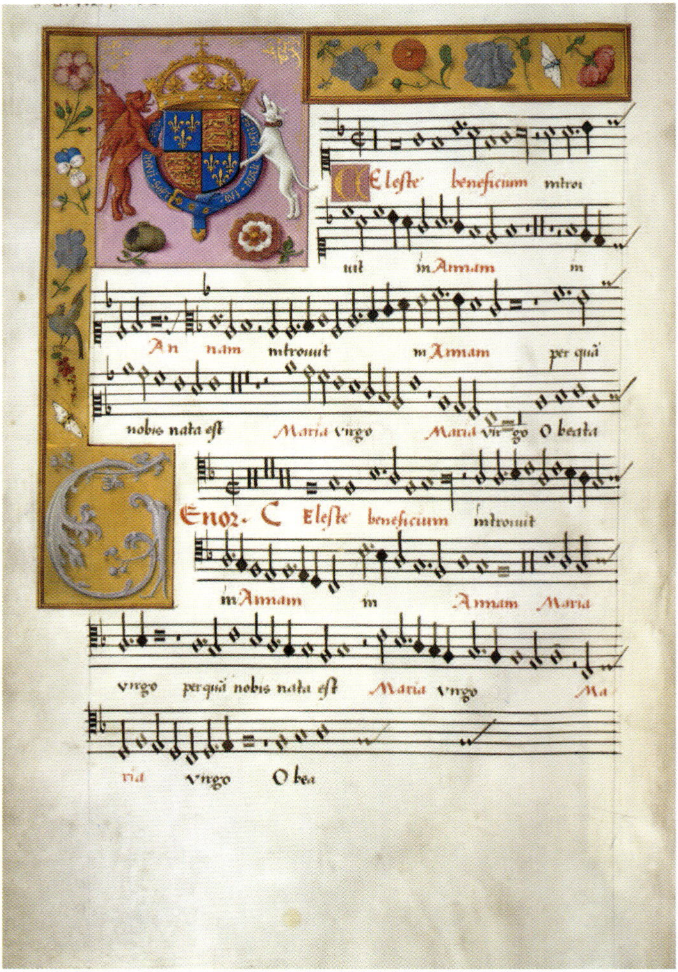

133 Border with the arms and devices of Henry VIII of England
Book of motets, made for Henry VIII of England
Workshop of Petrus Alamire
Mechelen, 1520s
375 × 260 mm
Royal MS 8 G vii, f. 2v

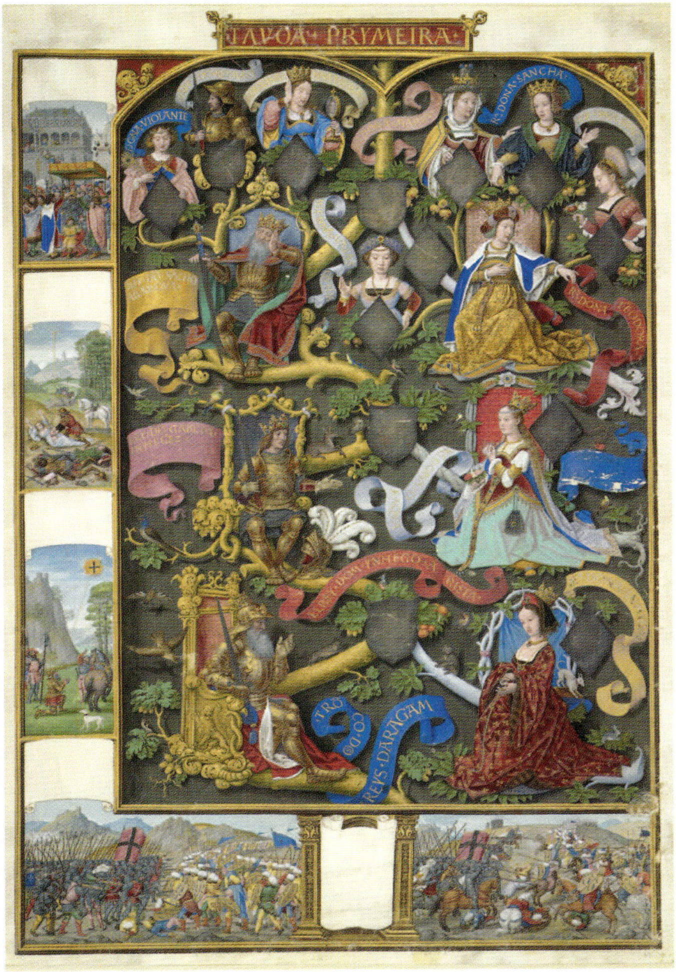

134 *Genealogical Tree of the Kings of Aragon*
Genealogy of Dom Fernando of Portugal
Simon Bening
Bruges, 1530–1534
559 × 394 mm
Add. MS 12531, f. 4

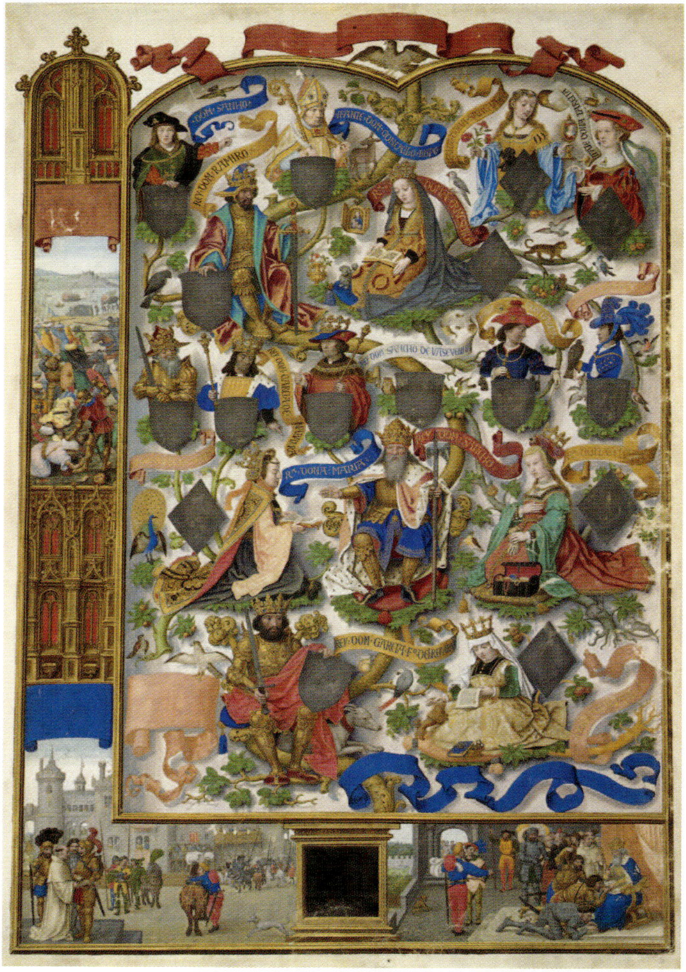

135 *Genealogical Tree of the Kings of Aragon*
Genealogy of Dom Fernando of Portugal
Simon Bening
Bruges, 1530–1534
559 × 394 mm
Add. MS 12531, f. 5

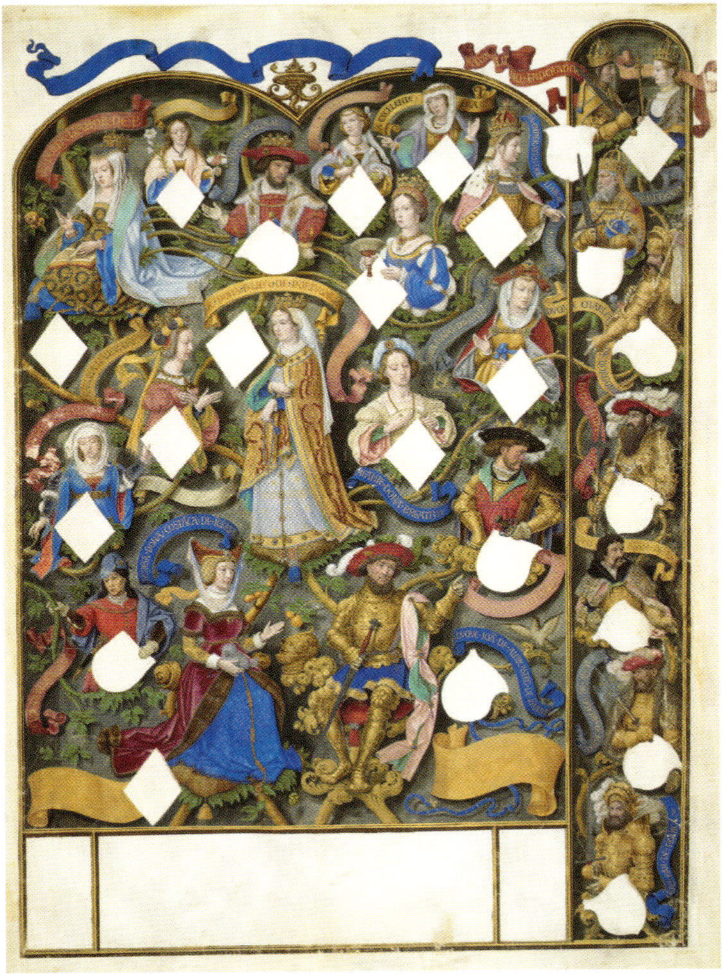

136 *Genealogical Tree of John, Duke of Lancaster*
Genealogy of Dom Fernando of Portugal
Simon Bening
Bruges, 1530–1534
559 × 394 mm
Add. MS 12531, f. 10

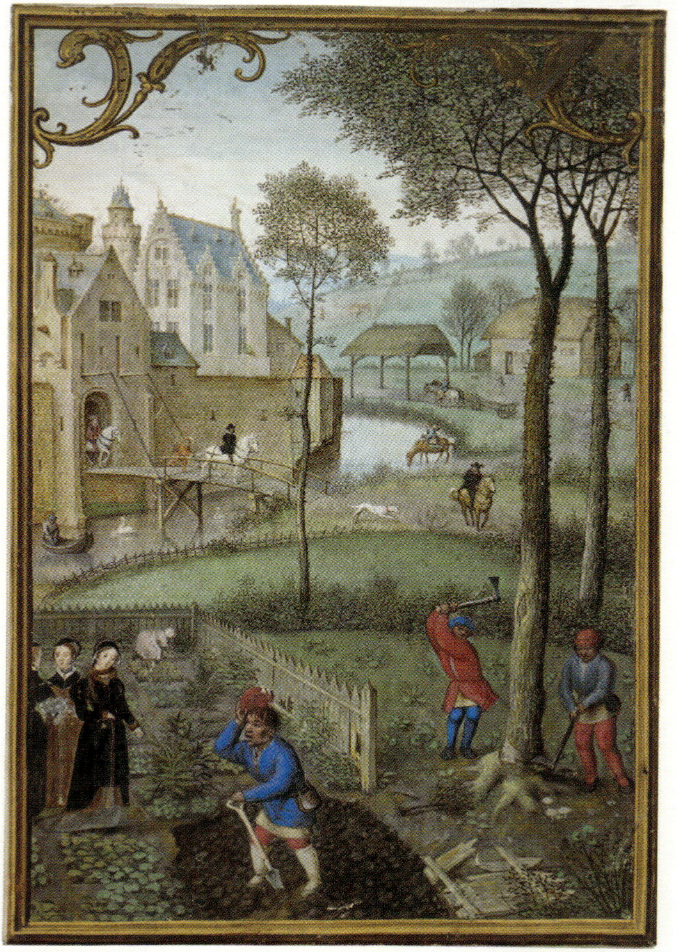

137 *March*
Simon Bening
Bruges, *c.* 1540–1550
152 × 102 mm
Add. MS 18855, f. 108

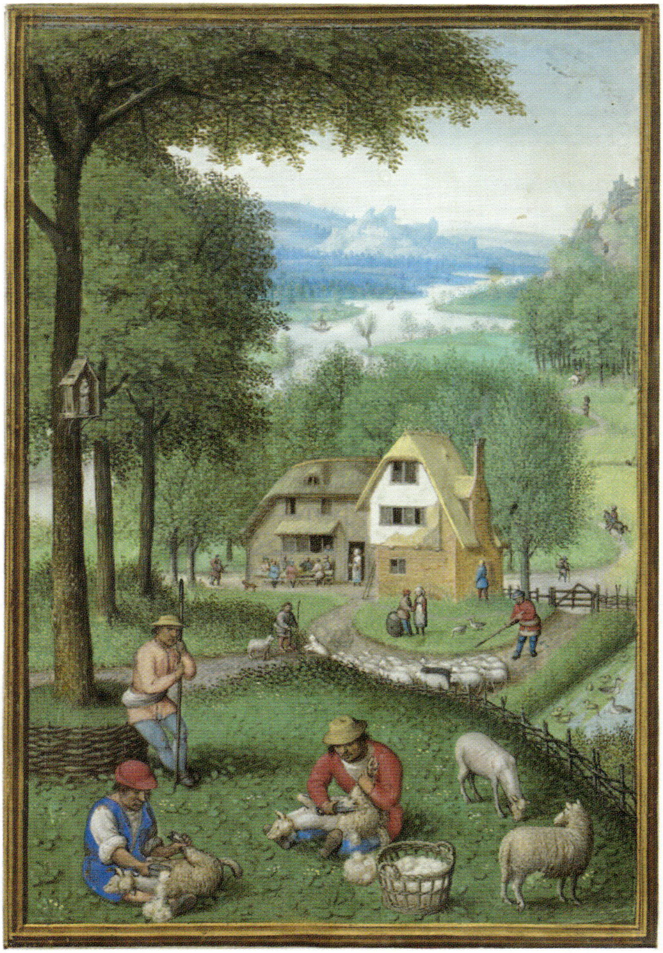

138 June
Simon Bening
Bruges, *c.* 1540–1550
152 × 102 mm
Add. MS 18855, f. 109

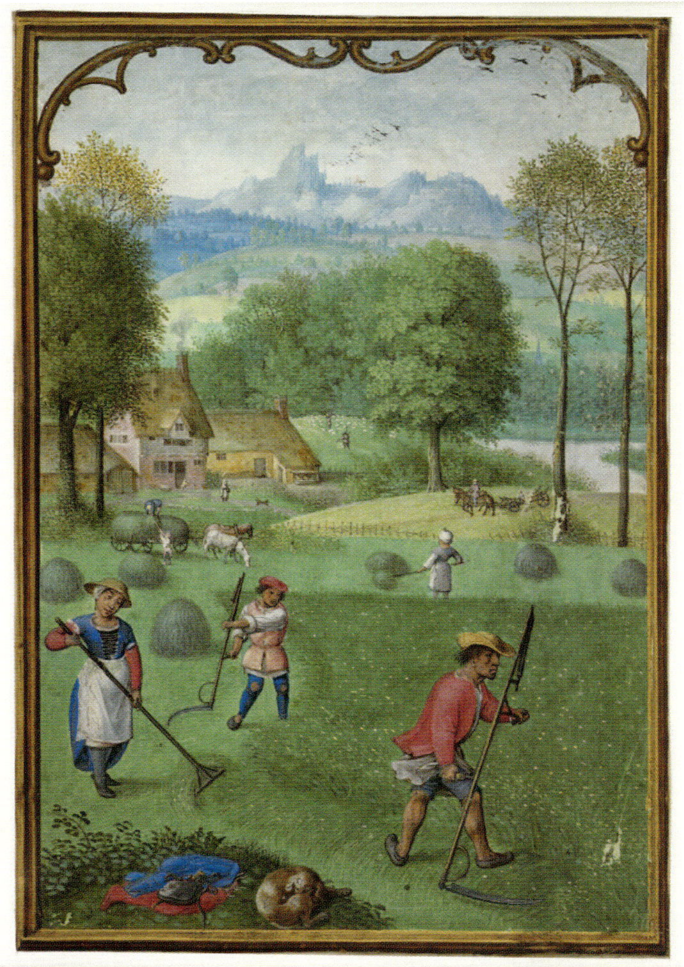

139 *July*
Simon Bening
Bruges, *c.* 1540–1550
152 × 102 mm
Add. MS 18855, f. 109v

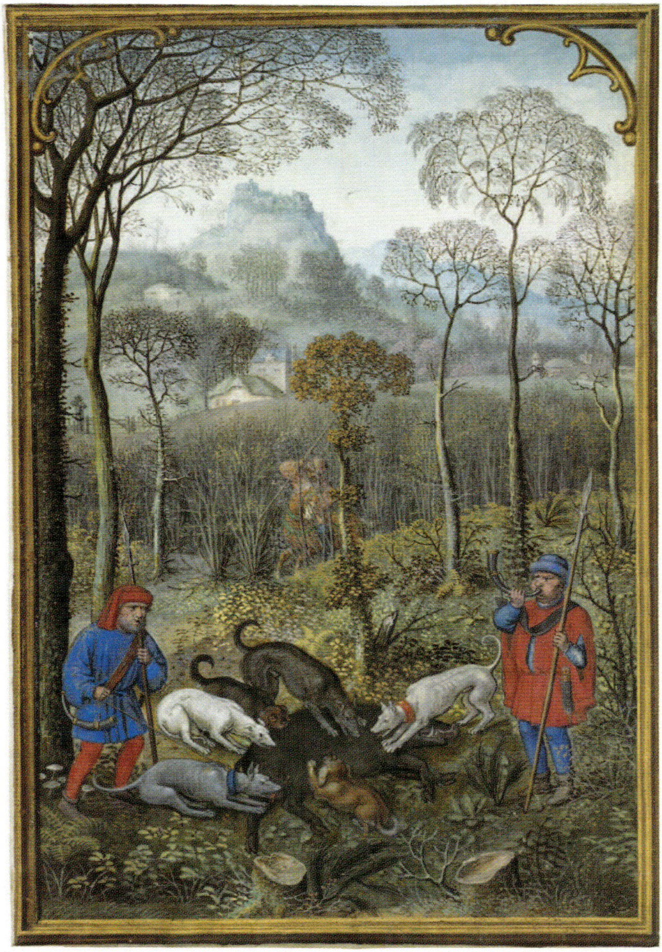

140 *December*
Simon Bening
Bruges, *c.* 1540–1550
152 × 102 mm
Add. MS 18855, f. 108v

Further Reading

FRIEDRICH WINKLER
Die flämische Buchmalerei des XV. und XVI. Jahrhunderts. Künstler und Werke von den Brüdern van Eyck bis zu Simon Bening.
Leipzig: E. A. Seeman, 1925. 2nd edn. Amsterdam: B.M. Israël, 1978.

OTTO PÄCHT
The Master of Mary of Burgundy.
London: Phaidon, 1948.

L. M. J. DELAISSÉ
La miniature flamande. Le mécénat de Philippe le Bon.
Brussels: Bibliothèque royale de Belgique, 1959.

THOMAS KREN (ed.)
Renaissance Painting in Manuscripts. Treasures from the British Library.
New York: Hudson Hills Press, 1983.

DAGMAR THOSS
Flämische Buchmalerei. Handschriftenschätze aus dem Burgunderreich.
Graz: Adeva, 1987.

MARK EVANS
The Sforza Hours.
London: The British Library, 1992.

THOMAS KREN (ed.)
Margaret of York, Simon Marmion and the Visions of Tondal.
Malibu: J. Paul Getty Museum, 1992.

ALAIN ARNOULD AND JEAN MICHEL MASSING (eds.)
Splendours of Flanders. Late Medieval Art in Cambridge Collections.
Cambridge: University Press, 1993.

JANET BACKHOUSE
The Isabella Breviary.
London: The British Library, 1993.

ERIK INGLIS
Hours of Mary of Burgundy. Codex Vindobonensis 1857, Vienna Österreichische Nationalbibliothek.
London: Harvey Miller, 1995.

JANET BACKHOUSE
The Hastings Hours.
London: The British Library, 1996.

BODO BRINKMANN
Die flämische Buchmalerei am Ende des Burgunderreichs. Der Meister des Dresdener Gebetbuchs und die Miniaturisten seiner Zeit.
Turnhout: Brepols, 1997.

SUSIE NASH
Between France and Flanders: Manuscript Painting in Amiens in the Fifteenth Century.
London: The British Library, 1999.

MAURITS SMEYERS (transl. by Karen Bowen and Dirk Imhof)
Flemish Miniatures from the 8th to the mid-16th century: The Medieval World on Parchment.
Turnhout: Brepols, 1999.

THOMAS KREN AND SCOT MCKENDRICK (eds.)
Illuminating the Renaissance: The Triumph of Flemish Manuscript Painting in Europe.
Los Angeles: J. Paul Getty Museum, 2003.

Index of Manuscripts

Numbers in brackets refer to plates in this book

Arundel MS 71 (18, 78)

Arundel MS 93 (79)

Burney MS 169 (19)

Cotton MS Augustus A v (35)

Cotton MS Augustus A vi (10)

Cotton MS Tiberius A ii (30)

Cotton MS Vespasian B i (20)

Harley MS 1211 (11)

Harley MS 2846 (9)

Harley MS 2897 (4)

Harley MS 2967 (29)

Harley MS 4379 (25–6)

Harley MS 4418 (7)

Harley MS 4425 (93)

Harley MS 6199 (59–60)

Royal MS 1 E v (112)

Royal MS 2 A xviii (1)

Royal MS 8 G vii (133)

Royal MS 11 E xi (111)

Royal MS 14 D vi (36)

Royal MS 14 E i (46)

Royal MS 14 E ii (62)

Royal MS 14 E v (63)

Royal MS 15 D i (45)

Royal MS 15 D iv (33)

Royal MS 15 E i (67

Royal MS 15 E iii (80)

Royal MS 15 E iv (65–6)

Royal MS 16 F ii (94)

Royal MS 16 G iii (43)

Royal MS 16 G viii (27)

Royal MS 17 F ii (47)

Royal MS 17 F iii (61)

Royal MS 17 F iv (24)

Royal MS 17 F v (84)

Royal MS 17 F vii (68)

Royal MS 18 D ii (119)

Royal MS 18 D ix (48)

Royal MS 18 D x (49)

Royal MS 18 E ii (64)

Royal MS 18 E iii (50)

Royal MS 18 E v (28)

Royal MS 19 C viii (106)
Royal MS 19 E iii (92)
Royal MS 20 C iii (83)
Royal MS 20 E i (91)
Yates Thompson MS 4 (12)
Yates Thompson MS 32 (82)
Yates Thompson MS 33 (17)
Sloane MS 2683 (2)
Add. MS 7970 (21–2)
Add. MS 11863 (44)
Add. MS 12531 (134–6)
Add. MS 15427 (127–8)
Add. MS 15469 (23)
Add. MS 16969 (77)
Add. MS 17026 (71–2)
Add. MS 17280 (73–6)
Add. MS 17440 (81)
Add. MS 17971 (8)
Add. MS 18851 (85–90)
Add. MS 18852 (97–100)
Add. MS 18855 (137–40)
Add. MS 19720 (58)
Add. MS 19738 (34)
Add. MS 20698 (31)
Add. MS 22567 (101–2)
Add. MS 24098 (129–32)
Add. MS 27948 (3)
Add. MS 31835 (5–6)
Add. MS 31838 (103–5)
Add. MS 34294 (120–6)
Add. MS 35313 (113–4)
Add. MS 35314 (95–6)
Add. MS 36619 (32)
Add. MS 38126 (51–6)
Add. MS 54782 (37–42)
Add. MS 71117 (13–6)
Egerton MS 1065 (57)
Egerton MS 1147 (109–10, 115–6)
Egerton MS 1149 (107–8)
Egerton MS 2045 (69–70)
Egerton MS 2125 (117–8)

For my parents

First published in 2003 by
The British Library
96 Euston Road
London NW1 2DB

British Library Cataloguing in Publication Data
A catalogue record is available from The British Library

ISBN 0 7123 4805 0

Designed and typeset by Andrew Shoolbred

Printed and bound in Singapore by Craft Print International